Europe's Future

Decoupling and Reforming

Sergio Fabbrini proposes a way out of the EU's crises, which have triggered an unprecedented cleavage between 'sovereignist' and 'Europeanist' forces. The intergovernmental governance of the multiple crises of the past decade has led to a division on the very rationale of Europe's integration project. Sovereignism (the expression of nationalistic and populist forces) has demanded more decision-making autonomy for the EU member states, although Europeanism has struggled to make an effective case against this challenge. Fabbrini proposes a new perspective to release the EU from this predicament, involving the decoupling and reforming of the EU: on the one hand, the economic community of the single market (consisting of the current member states of the EU and of others interested in joining or re-joining it); and on the other, the political union (largely based on the eurozone reformed according to an original model of the federal union).

Sergio Fabbrini is Dean of the Political Science Department and Professor of Political Science and International Relations at the LUISS Guido Carli University in Rome.

Europe's Future

Decoupling and Reforming

SERGIO FABBRINI
LUISS Guido Carli University of Rome

CAMBRIDGE
UNIVERSITY PRESS

CAMBRIDGE
UNIVERSITY PRESS

University Printing House, Cambridge CB2 8BS, United Kingdom

One Liberty Plaza, 20th Floor, New York, NY 10006, USA

477 Williamstown Road, Port Melbourne, VIC 3207, Australia

314–321, 3rd Floor, Plot 3, Splendor Forum, Jasola District Centre, New Delhi – 110025, India

79 Anson Road, #06–04/06, Singapore 079906

Cambridge University Press is part of the University of Cambridge.

It furthers the University's mission by disseminating knowledge in the pursuit of education, learning, and research at the highest international levels of excellence.

www.cambridge.org
Information on this title: www.cambridge.org/9781108484510
DOI: 10.1017/9781108680981

First published 2019

Printed and bound in Great Britain by Clays Ltd, Elcograf S.p.A.

A catalogue record for this publication is available from the British Library.

ISBN 978-1-108-48451-0 Hardback
ISBN 978-1-108-72327-5 Paperback

Contents

Preface

The European Union (EU) has turned the corner of its existential crisis. It has shown itself to be resilient to, first, the euro crisis, then to the arrival in Europe of millions of political refugees and economic migrants, after that to the terrorist attacks in the heart of Europe's cities, and finally to the decision of British (or, more specifically, English) voters to take their country out of it. As if that were not enough, those crises intertwined with an unexpected change in the geo-political equilibria on which the integration project was historically based. A new form of nationalism has taken root on the other side of the Atlantic, ending (or at least scaling back) the long political cycle that started at the end of the Second World War, marked by the opening up of the international system and its governance through multilateral institutions. Notwithstanding its resilience, the EU has, however, shown the inadequacies of its governance structure in managing those crises. The financial crisis lasted much longer than on the other side of the Atlantic, and it left a continent deeply divided between the north and south; the migration crisis led to unilateral and controversial choices by individual national governments that called into question the internal solidarity of the EU member states; the security crisis showed the existence of strategic and institutional divisions among EU member states regarding the response to terrorism. The governance structure of the EU has guaranteed its resilience, but it has also led to its internal divisions. Why and how has this happened?

The EU is structured on a dual constitutional regime, supranational in the policies of the single market and intergovernmental in the policies concerning traditional core state powers. As the aforementioned crises affected the latter issues, the institutional inadequacy of the EU can be considered the outcome of the deficiency of the intergovernmental regime (although this does not imply we should assume that the supranational regime would have guaranteed a better outcome).

It was the intergovernmental governance of the multiple crises that led to the emergence of new divisions among EU member states and within each of them. Particularly, it led (for the first time) to a division across states on the very rationale of the integration project. On one side, nationalism and populism created a "holy alliance" under the banner of *sovereignism* in order to claim more national decision-making autonomy within the EU framework. In fact, the dramatic consequences of secession (from the EU) even for a country such as the United Kingdom have led to an interpretation of nationalism as sovereignism within the EU rather than secession from the EU. Post-Brexit sovereignists want to remain within the EU, although they aim to hollow it out (i.e., not only to remove many of its supranational prerogatives but also to weaken its rule-of-law foundations). They do not aim to disintegrate the EU per se or to dismantle the single market, but they want to repatriate competences from Brussels and reinvigorate national sovereignty (understood in illiberal terms). Sovereignist political forces have gained control of several national governments in eastern and central Europe and are becoming more and more influential in the political processes of several countries in western Europe (as in Italy). This sovereignism is represented mainly by Viktor Orban, re-elected prime minister of Hungary on April 8, 2018, for a third mandate, whose party (Fidesz) is a member of the main pro-EU political party (the European People's Party). On the other side, Europeanist forces have hesitated in opposing the holy alliance, limiting themselves to containing sovereignism rather than challenging it with a renewed vision of a political Europe. Indeed, Europeanism does not seem to have elaborated a vision of Europe able to recompose the divisions that have emerged in the current decade during multiple crises – with the sole exception of Emmanuel Macron, who became the president of France on May 7, 2017. In any case, all over Europe, a political divide has emerged between sovereignist and Europeanist forces that has clouded the traditional cleavage between left and right. A new political era is emerging on the old continent.

This book aims to advance a perspective to bring the EU out of its paralyzing divisions, contributing to the debate on Europe's future. On the basis of the analytical reconstruction of the transformations of the EU, it advances an argument for decoupling the latter into two separate organizations. To the strategy of hollowing the EU out from within, pursued by sovereignist forces, Europeanist forces might respond with the strategy of separating out, on the one hand, the economic community of the single market (consisting of all the current member states of the EU and other states interested in joining or re-joining it, as in the case of the United Kingdom) and, on the other hand, a political union (necessarily based on those member states at the core of the Eurozone and Schengen projects because they already share crucial components of national sovereignty) organized according to the model of a federal union. It is a strategy of simultaneous decoupling and reforming. In fact, the economic community can be based on an interstate treaty, relieved of the unnecessary supranational regulations and intrusions into national sovereignty. The federal union must instead be based on a political compact that celebrates the division of sovereignty between (a large number of) policies to be managed at the national level (self-rule) and (a limited number of) policies to be managed at the supranational level (shared rule). The federal union paradigm assumes that the European integration process and national democracy are in no way irreconcilable, if we stop thinking (on the one hand) of Europe as a substitute for the nation state or (on the other) as an enemy of the nation state. This book arises from dissatisfaction with the theoretical models around which European integration has been interpreted and, above all, with the dual governance structure that has driven its development. Contrary to what is assumed by those models, it is here argued that only the federal method can limit the powers of shared rule and increase those of self-rule.

Without decoupling the current EU and without creating a political union with federal features (a federal union), whose members should remain within the single market, the EU will find it difficult to deal with the sovereignist challenges. The existence of a smaller (but nonetheless representing, if it corresponds to the Eurozone, 330 million inhabitants) but more cohesive federal union than the current EU (although following different legal and constitutional criteria from those adopted up to now) will represent the basic premise to stabilize the continent, to curb sovereignist sentiments, and to fight xenophobic and illiberal movements that are spreading all over Europe. This book aims to be a contribution to looking afresh at Europe's future.

This book has been written for a broader audience than EU specialists, although it is not easy to write about the EU in a way that is understandable to a non-specialist readership. The EU seems deliberately designed not to be understood, with its acronyms (which I have tried to limit), its technicalities (which I have tried to simplify), and its esoteric language (which I have tried to avoid). However, the future of Europe is too important not to be the subject of a public debate. This book is organized in the following way: After an introduction that synthetizes the correlation between the multiple crises of the 2010s and intergovernmental governance, Chapter 1 reconstructs the institutional transformation of the EU from the 1957 Rome Treaties to the 2009 Lisbon Treaty, with the aim of identifying its dual governance structure. Contrary to the standard reading of the EU as a unitary organization, the chapter shows that the EU has come to be organized around a basic dual constitution or decision-making regime (supranational in the single market, intergovernmental in the policies that became part of the EU agenda after the end of the Cold War). Without acknowledging this dualism, and particularly the nature of the intergovernmental regime, it is impossible to understand the difficulty the post-Lisbon EU had to face during the multiple crises. Because these crises were subjected to intergovernmental management, Chapter 2 analyzes the logic of the intergovernmental governance in dealing with the euro and migration and security crises to show not only the resilience of the EU but also its weakness. Chapter 3 discusses the nature of the sovereignist forces that emerged powerfully during those crises (triggered by the intergovernmental logic) and their view of an (undefined) economic project of integration. At the same time, the chapter discusses the alternative political view of integration, traditionally defined as Europeanism. The aim of the chapter is to show the weakness of both sovereignist and Europeanist arguments, owing to their shared (albeit different) ambiguities. Chapter 4 discusses the statist bias that affects all the arguments in favor of political integration, thus advancing the alternative paradigm of a federal union as an anti-statist form of political aggregation of asymmetrical and differentiated states. Chapter 5 then applies the analysis developed previously to the debate on the future of Europe, delineating the rationale for the decoupling of the EU, i.e., the separation (within the single market framework) of the economic and political integration projects. Within the single market shared by all the EU member states and regulated by an interstate treaty, a project of a federal union should be pursued by those member states already involved in the most advanced integration programs. This federal union should be based on multiple separation of powers in order to solve the paradox of constructing a sovereign union of sovereign states. Finally, the conclusion summarizes the reasons why Europe's future should be plural and not singular.

Rome, June 6, 2018

Introduction: Multiple Crises and European Governance

Introduction

On March 25, 1957, six countries (Belgium, France, Germany, Italy, Luxembourg, and the Netherlands) signed the Treaties of Rome, on the basis of which (what we now call) the European Union (EU) was established. Since then, in Europe, there has been a constant process of institutional deepening of the integration process and its enlargement to new states. History has continued to blow wind into the sails of aggregation – so much so that for a long period there was a widespread belief, among elites as well as the public, that the outcome of the integration process would be the reconstruction of the whole continent within a single political organization, the United States of Europe. This was the cherished dream of pioneers of Europeanism such as Altiero Spinelli and Ernesto Rossi who, in their isolation at Ventotene, in 1941 wrote a *Manifesto for a Free and United Europe*. Since then, the formation of a European federation has been considered the necessary response to the demons of European nationalisms. Those demons led to two world wars and the material and moral destruction of Europe. At the start of the integration process, one motivation therefore prevailed over the others: guaranteeing peace on the continent. Without peace, it would not be possible to create the conditions for growth; without growth, it would be difficult to consolidate the young post-war national democracies. The EU is, in short, the institutional form that sought to reconcile the needs of peace, growth, and (political and social) democracy. Through the EU, those needs have been able to reinforce one another, giving rise to a positive-sum game to everyone's benefit. Of course, this process has passed through crisis after crisis. However, despite those crises, the EU has become institutionalized and has ended up aggregating almost all the European states.

Nonetheless, more than sixty years after the Treaties of Rome, the scenario for the integration process has changed dramatically. Starting in 2008, Europe has been submerged by a veritable tsunami: the financial crisis that soon became the crisis of the single currency, the euro, the real symbol of the move from an economic community to a union with political ends. No financial crisis has ever lasted as long. Then the euro crisis was joined by the migration crisis. The latter crisis peaked in the summer of 2015 when a million Syrian refugees crossed the EU's borders to flee the disastrous civil and religious war being waged in their country. This crisis was in turn heightened by the enormous movements of people from other areas of civil and religious conflict (Somalia, Eritrea, Libya, Yemen, Afghanistan), as well as from areas of extreme poverty (Saharan Africa). These crises then became even more intractable as they intertwined with repeated terrorist attacks of hitherto unheard of savagery in some European cities, such as the dramatic terrorist attack in Paris in November 2015, which followed another serious attack, again in Paris, at the start of 2015 (Caporaso 2018). Those crises, as Krastev (2017: 59) noted, constitute "a turning point in the political dynamics of the European project."

Given the EU's problems in effectively addressing the challenges arising from these multiple crises, at the end of the 2010s public opinion in its member states has swung in an increasingly nationalist direction. Nationalist movements and sentiments have taken hold everywhere, even if the demand to restore national policy-making power has taken different forms. It has been promoted and led by left-wing parties, such as in Greece and Spain; by right-wing parties, such as in France, Great Britain, Denmark, Poland, and Hungary; and by populist parties unattached to the traditional left/right axis in European politics, as in Italy. In the past, we have never seen the formation of such widespread anti-European movements in almost all the (then) twenty-eight member states of the EU. The pressure to regain control over domestic policies peaked with the United Kingdom's decision to leave the EU, after the referendum of June 23, 2016, a decision thus formalized on March 29, 2017. Thus, after exactly sixty years, during which the European agenda was built around the theme of enlargement (the request for integration into the EU of a growing number of countries, first from western Europe and then from the east), with Brexit the European agenda has changed significantly. The question has become how to manage the forces for disintegration (although not necessarily secession); it is no longer about how to regulate the requests for further integration.

Moreover, the arrival of Donald Trump to the presidency of the United States (US) in January 2017 has radically altered the transatlantic equilibrium on which the European integration process had been based since the 1957 Treaties of Rome. It was the US, emerged victorious from the world conflict, which enabled western European countries to move in the direction of a supranational integration. In the long post–Second World War period, it has been the US that (albeit with significant differences between one presidency and another and with not a few political interferences) played the crucial role of security's provider to Europe, both militarily (through its leadership of the North Atlantic Treaty Organization [NATO]) and politically (through its supervision over the continent's democratic evolution). This US leadership was thus crucial, after 1989, for healing the wounds of the Cold War between western and eastern Europe. There is no longer any guarantee of US determination to support the integration of the continent, nor its territorial integrity, particularly, to oppose Russia's expansionist goals on Europe's eastern borders, epitomized by its 2014 annexation of Crimea. With Brexit and the Trump presidency, a political cycle, which lasted well over half a century, has come to an end.

It is in this context that the analyses and proposals made in this book must be placed. It is a context that is unprecedented, despite the numerous crises faced by the EU in the past. The multiple crises of the 2010s have activated centrifugal forces that the EU has been unable to address with institutions capable of dealing with them. Certainly, the costs of Brexit dissipated the ambiguity of a plausible disintegration's alternative to integration. After Brexit, anti-Europeanists claim more sovereignty within the EU, with the aim of transforming the EU in an (undefined) organization of economic cooperation, rather than independence from the EU. This (although confused) challenge to the project of building "an ever closer union" (as the 1957 Rome Treaties' Preamble declared) has been met by the supporters of the latter through the re-affirmation of politics as usual, i.e., through either the functionalist approach of muddling-through or the intergovernmental approach of letting national governments find ad hoc solutions for ad hoc problems. Because of the lack of political courage and strategic thinking of its supporters, the EU has lost its sense of the future without at the same time acquiring awareness of the difficulties of the present. Europeanists have put their trust in the resistance of EU procedures, in the daily survival of cooperative practices between national governments, in the teleological assumption that integration is irreversible. In the meantime, anti-Europeanists continue to chip away at the integration process, using every difficulty to highlight its inadequacy to solve citizens' problems.

Neither sovereignists nor Europeanists understand, however, that the European crisis was, and still is, the consequence of the interplay between historical changes and inadequate institutions. It has taken the form of an institutional crisis but reflects indeed a crisis of vision on Europe's future. Because sovereignism and Europeanism have intrinsic weaknesses, it is necessary to think differently from the past, promoting an integration process that should meet different expectations. It is the strategy of promoting a constitutional distinction between an economic community and a federal union connected in the operation of the single market – a federal union based on a political compact and an economic community organized by an interstate treaty. Europe's future needs innovative institutional solutions. Here, I propose the argument developed in the subsequent chapters. First, I introduce my interpretation of the EU. Second, I describe the main crises that affected the EU. Third, I analyze the limits of the intergovernmental governance that managed those crises.

The Dual Constitution of the European Union

The multiple crises that the EU has had to face have occurred in policy areas outside the common market (which became the single or internal market with the Single European Act of 1986). Those crises have in fact occurred in the sectors of economic policy, law and home affairs, defense and security policy, policy sectors that were considered of common interest beginning with the Maastricht Treaty of 1992. At the Intergovernmental Conference that prepared the draft of that treaty, the decision was made to take an institutional break from the supranational system, which up to then had governed the integration of the single market. If the latter was taken forward by using the so-called community or supranational method, in Maastricht it was decided that the new policies should be Europeanized by using a new decision-making method, which was subsequently defined as intergovernmental.

In Maastricht, distinct organizations were created to manage them, organizations known as "pillars." An intergovernmental pillar was created to decide Common Foreign and Security Policy (CFSP), another intergovernmental pillar to decide policies linked to Justice and Home Affairs (JHA), and, finally, the intergovernmental method was introduced to decide on the economic policy (with the related fiscal and budget policies) of the Economic and Monetary Union (EMU, which I will call here the Eurozone), while monetary policy was instead entrusted to the independent control of the European Central Bank. The Lisbon Treaty of 2009 (constituted by three treaties: the Treaty on European Union, or TEU; the Treaty on the Functioning of the European Union, or TFEU; and the Charter of Fundamental Rights) abolished the pillars, but left in place the intergovernmental method by which to decide those policies.

With Maastricht, therefore, a dual constitution or decision-making regime was formed within the EU. As of 1992, the EU has therefore lost its unitarian, supranational character, as it had been defined by the founding Treaties of Rome of 1957. The regulatory policies of the single market have continued to be decided in accordance with the supranational method institutionalized in the Treaties of Rome: The European Commission (which holds a monopoly over legislative initiative) puts a legislative proposal (either a regulation or a directive) to the Council of Ministers (the Council of the EU), which votes on a qualified majority basis and (increasingly) to the European Parliament (which votes on a simple majority basis). In the supranational EU of the single market, the European Parliament has emerged as the institution that has increased its powers the most, even at the expense of the Commission (Kreppel and Oztas 2016), to the extent that the Lisbon Treaty of 2009 formalized its role as co-legislator in almost all the regulatory policies of the single market. The approval of the Commission's proposals by both the Council of Ministers and the European Parliament has become, with the Lisbon Treaty, the ordinary legislative procedure of the single market. The latter has continued to function through legislative proceedings (known as integration through law), acts taking the form of regulations (which must then be implemented as they are by the member states) and directives (which set the objectives to be achieved, leaving the decision on how to achieve them to the member states). Of course, there has been no lack of resistance to the extension of the single market to delicate areas for individual member states (such as that of services). Nonetheless, in these policies, there has been no crisis. Quite the opposite. Just think of the infraction procedure launched in autumn 2016 by the Commission against an IT giant such as Apple, accused of having violated the rules of competition in benefiting tax discounts from the Irish government.

The crisis, on the other hand, has been seen in the policies governed by the intergovernmental method. The intergovernmental method was chosen by national governments to decide policies linked to the core state powers (Genschel and Jachtenfuchs 2014), i.e., policies that were traditionally at the heart of national sovereignty and jealously controlled by national governments. Because these are policies of strategic importance (to the extent that they are often called strategic policies, a term that I will use, too), national governments wanted to control them. In the intergovernmental EU, the decision-making axis is structured around the relationship between the European Council and the Council of Ministers. In particular, the European Council of heads of state and government (from here onward, only heads of government) has become the predominant institution, moreover formally recognized for the first time as an EU institution by the Lisbon Treaty. In these intergovernmental policies, integration consists of the voluntary coordination of member state governments, with the consequence of downsizing the legislative role of the European Parliament and the supervisory role of the European Court of Justice, limiting the Commission to a technical (as opposed to political) role.

As a default condition, while the supranational method involves deciding on a majority basis, the intergovernmental method instead involves deciding on a unanimity basis. Unanimity means that each governmental leader or minister taking part in the deliberative process has an acknowledged power of veto. That power of veto cannot be permanently threatened without calling into question the consensual logic that must prevail within the Council of Ministers and above all the European Council. Intergovernmental deliberation presupposes reciprocal trust among the national governments and requires their political commitment to find policy solutions that can meet the legitimate needs of each of them (Puetter 2014; Wessels 2015). However, in times of crisis, intergovernmental deliberation struggles to work. Crises tend to impact national interests, because their solutions have inevitable implications in terms of the distribution of resources or costs (Genschel and Jachtenfuchs 2017). Because the multiple crises of the 2010s have occurred in the field of intergovernmental policies, their persistence must be connected to the intergovernmental method for managing them. That method has exacerbated the crises instead of calming them down. Intergovernmental governance, which had in fact worked under the ordinary pre-2008 conditions, could not withstand the extraordinary post-2008 conditions (Joerges 2016). The choice made in Maastricht thus came to a head with the crises that followed in the second decade of the twenty-first century.

The Development of Multiple Crises

The prolonged crisis of the euro and the inability of intergovernmental governance to manage the crisis have led to a change in the political equilibria of the member states of the Eurozone, also due to the hardening of the unrest among their electorates. Several serving governments had to resign because of their inability to comply with the restrictions of intergovernmental governance, or they were replaced in elections held in a political climate that had become increasingly anti-European. The divisions between the states of northern and southern Europe have increased without the possibility of a democratic reconciliation (Hacker and Koch 2017). Just recall the referendum of July 5, 2015, held in Greece, superficially called by that country's government on the austerity measures it would have to adopt to obtain the third package of financial aid needed to prevent its defaulting. Despite the clear result of that referendum (around two-thirds of the electorate voted against those austerity measures), the Greek government was then forced to reverse its anti-austerity position at the extraordinary meeting of the European Council of July 12 or risk making the country insolvent. The reaction of the Eurozone to the Greek referendum dramatically showed the strength of external constraints (on a country) in a highly interdependent economic and monetary system (such as the Eurozone). In intergovernmental governance, there should be no room for national unilateral claims, only reciprocal control among the national governments – even though the power of control may quite easily be unfairly distributed.

The same happened with the policies to manage the enormous migration flows heading toward Europe. For a long time, the countries that were most exposed to these flows, such as Italy and Greece, were left alone to handle them on the basis of the Dublin Regulation of 2003, under which the country of first arrival has the duty to recognize migrants and, if necessary, send them back to their country of origin. As early as 2013, Italy, without significant EU financial support, took on the responsibility (with its Mare Nostrum operation) of facing up to the dramatic humanitarian emergency of migrants who were crossing the Mediterranean without any regard for their own safety. This situation worsened enormously in subsequent years, albeit (thanks to the Mare Nostrum operation then replaced by the Triton operation backed by the EU) part of the migration flows were blocked, flows which then shifted to a land-based route (connecting Syria with Turkey and then the Balkan states to reach the eastern borders of the EU). Very soon these migration flows created defensive reactions in the countries of first arrival. Starting with Hungary and then involving Slovenia and Croatia, the governments of those countries immediately started to build barriers and walls on their borders. In their turn, France and Germany and other countries suspended, or threatened to suspend, the free circulation of people in the so-called Schengen area (from the name of the town where an international agreement was signed in 1985 between five European countries to abolish checks on people at their borders, an agreement which then became a primary law of the EU with the Amsterdam Treaty of 1999). However, fences rarely manage to keep the water out. Migrants found other ways to reach the developed countries of Europe (and, above all, to reach the richest of them).

If the financial crisis led to a cleavage between the south and the north of the Eurozone, a new cleavage has occurred between the states of western and eastern Europe over the policy for handling refugees and so promoting their redistribution within the EU member states. When in September 2015 the Commission put to the Council a proposal to distribute 120,000 refugees among the various member states, a proposal then approved on a qualified majority basis by the Council of Ministers at its September 22 meeting, the entire block of eastern countries declared that decision illegitimate (albeit qualified majority voting was envisaged in the field of asylum policies). Because that decision had an uncertain legal character, as do all intergovernmental decisions, no mechanism could oblige national governments to implement it. The intergovernmental method can therefore lead to the nullification of its own deliberations. After all, asylum policy, as with fiscal and budgetary policy, has a strong domestic impact. Indeed, the migration flows in Europe have activated parties and movements to oppose them, which have gathered increasing electoral consensus. The refusal to accept political refugees for domestic electoral reasons (which, according to international law, and not just that of Europe, is unjustifiable), as well as opposing economic migration, has brought votes to parties that are openly anti-EU. Because Schengen had abolished internal borders without protecting external borders, it was easy to argue that the growth in migration was due to the integration process. Not only in almost all the countries of the east but also in countries of the north, the EU has become the scapegoat for every unwelcome phenomenon. Migration flows have added fuel to the fire of the various forms of nationalism.

The dramatic terrorist attacks on European soil, particularly that in Paris on November 13, 2015, which followed the previous attack in the same city on January 7, 2015, also showed the difficulty the EU has in acting cohesively and coherently in terms of security. Immediately after the attack, the French government used Art. 42.7 of the TEU, which requires member states to provide help and assistance to another member state that has suffered armed attack on its own soil. This article refers to member states and not to the EU as such. The EU has not even recognized the task of coordinating the action of the member states. France could have used Art. 222 of the TFEU, which envisages, in the case of terrorist attacks against a member state, an obligation for the EU (as an organization) to intervene. However, the then French president François Hollande decided to use Art. 42.7 of the TEU, which preserves national prerogatives in the field of security and defense, whereas if Art. 222 of the TFEU had been used, France would have had to coordinate its own action with the other member states and with the supranational institutions. In the latter case, it would have been possible to create the conditions to start a Permanent Structured Cooperation (PESCO) in the field of security and defense, a possibility envisaged by the Lisbon Treaty, regularly promised since the joint Franco-British Saint-Malo declaration of 1998 (and the consequent creation of the European Common Security and Defence Policy, or CSDP) but unrealized for twenty years. The result was that France found itself alone, in the EU, in organizing the military response to terrorism. The French bombing of the positions of the Islamic State in Syria was supported mainly by non-European countries (such as the US and Russia), rather than by EU countries (with the partial and limited exception of the United Kingdom). Only with the arrival to the French presidency of Emmanuel Macron in May 2017 and the departure of the

United Kingdom from the EU was it possible to inaugurate the first PESCO in defense and security in December 2017. However, because twenty-five of the twenty-seven EU member states agreed to participate in PESCO, it seems reasonable to assume that the interstate divisions, which had paralyzed the EU in the past, will probably also reemerge within the new program of permanent structured cooperation.

The Intergovernmental Implosion

The multiple crises that occurred in the second decade of the twenty-first century have led to an increasing administrative centralization of decision-making as a response to the decisional paralysis caused by intergovernmental deliberations, a paralysis due to the reciprocal lack of trust between the various national governments heightened by those crises. Although the European Council played the role of crisis manager, that management highlighted structural incongruences of the intergovernmental governance. In the intergovernmental governance, there is confusion over the distinction in responsibilities and prerogatives between the European and national levels. This has been particularly evident in economic policy. Because the decision-making process must be based on reciprocal consensus and trust among the member states, if these no longer exist then a highly intrusive mechanism of administrative centralization and judicial supervision over national prerogatives would be necessarily introduced. Instead of separating between the levels of government and their respective decision-making responsibilities, in the Eurozone the opposite strategy was pursued, which entrusts to a center with no electoral legitimacy the duty of controlling, if not determining, the fiscal choices of the member states. The intergovernmental governance implies a direct connection between national and supranational politics, with a double consequence. Single national parliaments cannot call into question a decision made by an organ (the European Council) to which the governmental leader expressing the parliamentary majority in each of them also belongs. At the same time, national idiosyncrasies can be transferred directly into the supranational level. One has only to think about what would have happened if Marine Le Pen, and not Emmanuel Macron, had become the president of France (and thus a member of the European Council). The confusion between the various levels of government has led to a decision-making system without checks and balances, operating on the basis of administrative mechanisms, where the loss of national democratic sovereignty has not been balanced by increased democratic sovereignty at the European level.

Particularly in conditions of crisis, it is unlikely that the intergovernmental governance produces legitimate and effective decisions. Because strategic policies have redistributive effects, it is difficult to create consensus in the decision-making process when national interests are in conflict. In fact, national governments, during the euro crisis or the migration crises, threatened to use their power of veto or watered down the domestic implementation of undesired decisions. Because the crises with redistributive effects can call into question crucial domestic political equilibria, the intergovernmental governance incentivizes the strongest member states to act unilaterally in order to escape the unanimity constraints. This has happened by degrees and with a range of effects (Fabbrini 2016a). In the Eurozone's economic policy, a German *directoire* was established for protecting German interests (and German money) (Jacoby 2017). The legislative measures (European Semester, Six Pack, and Two Pack) and the intergovernmental agreements (European Stability Mechanism, Fiscal Compact, Single Resolution Fund for banking crises) decided during the euro crisis created the institutional and cognitive conditions for the exercise of German leadership. Such leadership, however, was challenged by the governments of the southern European states (particularly by the Italian governments of the period 2013–2018), with the increasingly explicit support of Commission president Jean-Claude Juncker. It was more difficult instead to form a permanent *directoire* in the two other strategic policy areas. In migration and asylum policy, the German position was openly challenged by various countries from eastern Europe, with the growing explicit support of the then president of the European Council itself, the Pole Donald Tusk. Not only was the principle of quotas queried, but also the creation of a European Border and Coast Guard (EBCG), following a proposal of the Commission, was watered down. The EBCG, launched officially in October 2016, is certainly based on more resources and staff than those available for the previous Frontex program; however, it is expected to integrate national border defense bodies but is not authorized to operate autonomously from them.

Moreover, the resistance of this or that national government to collegial decisions, which might penalize it domestically, drove the strongest countries to find extra-institutional solutions. For example, at the height of the Syrian refugee crisis, in September 2015, the German government sought solutions outside the European Council through the formation of a coalition of the willing (to help it manage the enormous flow of refugees arriving in Germany). Moreover, given the resistance encountered domestically to its choice of providing an unconditional welcome to refugees, the German government therefore started bilateral diplomacy with Turkey. This led to an agreement with Turkey, later formalized by the European Council. The deal with the Turkish government, aimed at blocking the Balkan road, redirected the flow of refugees and migrants toward the Mediterranean road, connecting Libya to Italy and Greece, redistributing the costs of the migration policy to the latter countries. In turn, Italy went for a similar strategy when it decided to deal directly with Libyan authorities, reaching an agreement, in the summer of 2017, with the tribes controlling the road of the migrants toward the Mediterranean. Unofficially, those tribes were paid for keeping the migrants in Libyan territory, rewarding them more than they could receive from criminal organizations trafficking in persons and migrant smuggling. The deal functioned, diminishing the number of migrants trying to cross the Mediterranean, although many of them were kept in camps that disrespected basic human rights principles in their management. Regardless of the merits of decisions made by the German or Italian government, the idea of coalitions of willing countries as well as that of bilateral diplomacy have ended up further delegitimizing the system of intergovernmental governance.

The same happened in the case of the response to terrorism. France recovered its centrality in defense and security policy, albeit at the price of remaining relatively isolated from the other member states of the EU. The operation that was undertaken in Libya in 2011, i.e., the formation of a European military coalition led by a Franco-British *directoire* and supported by NATO (Fabbrini 2014), with the purpose of ending Gaddafi's political regime, was not repeated in 2015. Starting with Italy, various member states of the EU provided assistance to France, without, however, sharing its military fate. Indeed, in the Libyan crisis, France and Italy supported different political coalitions. In short, the intergovernmental approach has produced divisions between states (between countries of the north and south of the Eurozone during the euro crisis, between countries of the west and east during the migration crisis, between countries with different military and geo-economic interests during the security crisis) such as has never happened before in the long integration process. Regarding the interstate divisions triggered by the euro crisis, Bastasin (2015) talked of the first European war of interdependence.

Conclusion

The multiple crises of the 2010s have proven the inadequacy of the model of intergovernmental governance adopted by the EU to handle strategic policies (such as economic policy, home affairs policy, and security and defense policy). The high political salience of the crises' issues has led to their politicization. The EU has moved from the permissive consensus of the past to a new constraining dissensus (to use concepts from Hooghe and Marks 2009). That politicization has encouraged centrifugal forces in almost all the member states of the EU, forces seeking to take back national control over strategic policies and, more generally, to reduce the competences and role of the EU. However, given the inability of the EU to manage the financial crisis or to address migration flows or to respond to terrorist attacks, there has been an inevitable push from public opinion seeking a return of those policies to the national level. Because it was not possible to make an impact on the public policies and workings of the EU, the dissatisfaction of citizens has come to the fore in national elections, with the effect of voting down incumbent governments although they were not individually responsible for the collegial choices made by the intergovernmental institutions. Because the citizens of the countries more affected by the crises could not identify mechanisms to influence EU decisions, a growing number of them turned to nationalist solutions to guarantee their economic, political, and military security. Certainly, the elections for the European Parliament provided a channel to transfer dissatisfaction into the EU. However, owing to the limited powers of the European Parliament over the policies relating to the multiple crises, that dissatisfaction has not had an impact on the political direction of the EU.

Certainly, national electors expressed their dissatisfaction with varying degrees. Consider the main Eurozone member states. In the Italian parliamentary elections of March 4, 2018, sovereignist forces (League and Five Star) won (together) more than 50 percent of the vote; in the first round of the French presidential elections of April 23, 2017, sovereignist candidates (Marine Le Pen and Jean-Luc Mélenchon) got more than 40 percent of the vote; in Germany, in the 2017 federal elections for the Bundestag, the sovereignist party, *Alternative für Deutschland*, or AfD, won 12.6 percent of the vote and received 94 seats, becoming the third party in the country. This variance was an effect of the asymmetries of the Eurozone's policies, closer to the preferences of mainstream German voters than to those of the mainstream Italian or French voters. In central and eastern Europe, dissatisfaction was the result of an EU considered too intrusive in national prerogatives. This dissatisfaction led sovereignist forces and candidates to become the main governmental actors in the Visegrad Group (Poland, Hungary, the Czech Republic, and Slovakia), as well as in Austria (after the parliamentary elections of October 15, 2017). Across Europe, after Brexit, nationalist political forces have started to reframe their strategy, claiming more national sovereignty (on issues considered crucial by the incumbent government) but without threatening to leave the EU altogether. As shown by the April 8, 2018, Hungarian parliamentary elections, in which the incumbent governing party (the sovereignist Fidesz) received 48 percent of vote on an electoral platform strongly critical of the EU policies and authority but run from within the main pro-EU political party (the European People's Party). In general, every national or subnational election has seen the growing establishment of sovereignist parties or movements, albeit internally differentiated in terms of their ideological origin or cultural positioning. Sovereignism has become the alternative to Europeanism, merging the criticism of the supranational project (at what the EU is) with the criticism of the specific policies pursued by the EU (at what the EU does). In sum, the multiple crises of the 2010s have raised the problem of the reform of the EU. Because the cure for the defects of the intergovernmental approach will not likely be found in the traditional supranational approach, then a new governance model needs to be elaborated for governing the strategic policies entered into the EU agenda with the 1992 Maastricht Treaty.

1 | *Supranational and Intergovernmental Governance*

Introduction

The EU is the result of a long historical process of voluntary integration among nation states that had been independent for centuries. For the first time in Europe's long history, a process of this type has gained ground. All previous attempts at aggregating European states had been driven by force, never by consensus. The Second World War created political, and not merely historical, discontinuity in Europe. After the war, in western Europe, liberal democracies returned and, with them, the political forms of mass mobilization and electoral participation. All this was due to the active support of the US (the western winners of the war), support which was economic and political, as well as cultural. And, above all, it was due to the formation of a military alliance of European countries led by the US (the North Atlantic Treaty Organization, or NATO, set up in Washington, DC, in 1949), which solved the historical dilemma of security in Europe. In the desperate climate following the Second World War, new national leadership had come to the fore in the main European countries, new because there was finally an awareness of the dangers of nationalism. The Soviet threat, from behind the Iron Curtain, was, in turn, a formidable incentive for the countries of western Europe to find advanced forms of integration. It is in that context that we must place the creation of what we today call the EU.

The national elites that promoted the EU had one key objective – to create a pact for peace among countries that had historically been at war, on condition that it would be more sound to the extent it was supported by matching widespread economic growth. Peace and well-being were seen (by men such as Robert Schuman, Alcide De Gasperi, and Konrad Adenauer) as the conditions to smooth over the warlike instincts of nationalism, and so to consolidate the new constitutional democracies that emerged in the defeat of the latter. Economic modernization had become the condition of political democratization. However, the end of the Cold War (between 1989 and 1991) raised new challenges for European integration, starting with the reunification of Germany in the autumn of 1990 and ending with the removal of Soviet control over the countries of eastern Europe. Faced with these historic changes, the EU could no longer limit itself to regulating the single market but had to come to grips with policies that had traditionally been at the heart of national sovereignty. So, at Maastricht those policies were Europeanized, but in accordance with a method that would enable national governments to control their policy making. Intergovernmental pillars were then created to manage them. Through these pillars, the unitary character of the organization that emerged from the Treaties of Rome of 1957 was thus impaired. Particularly since the Maastricht Treaty, a process of policy and institutional differentiation has developed within the EU. Nevertheless, this differentiation has come to be ordered around two stable decision-making regimes, the supranational and the intergovernmental. Thus, contrary to the standard interpretation (Borzel 2016: 12) of "the EU's governance [according to which the latter] has evolved over time developing different varieties of inter- and trans-governmental negotiation and regulatory competition in the shadow of supranational hierarchy," this chapter instead argues that the EU has passed through a process of institutionalization, ending up in formalizing distinct decision-making regimes, although transitory forms of inter- and trans-governmental governance patterns have emerged. The chapter first reconstructs the period of market-building. Second, it discusses the changes developed between the 1992 Maastricht Treaty and the 2009 Lisbon Treaty. Third and fourth, it identifies the institutional features of the two decision-making regimes (supranational and intergovernmental) finally institutionalized by the latter treaty. The conclusion summarizes the argument that the process of the EU's institutionalization was accompanied by two contrasting governance systems (although combinations of the two can be detected in micro-policy fields).

The First Decades of Integration

The EU was created in 1957 in Rome as a project for the construction of an integrated market on a continental scale, even if the first seeds of integration were sown by the 1952 treaties setting up both the European Coal and Steel Community (ECSC) and the European Defence Community (EDC), two arms (one economic and the other political) of the same project. It was, however, inevitable that the EU developed from a project of economic integration, after the French Assembly of the IV Republic voted against the EDC project in 1954. After that vote, the main leaders of (continental and western) Europe decided to promote political integration through economic integration (Dinan 2005). Nonetheless, there is no doubt (Judt 2005) that these leaders interpreted the creation of the European Economic Community, envisaged by the 1957 Treaties of Rome, as a response to the need to end a long era of civil wars on the European continent. The EU thus came into being as a peace pact among the countries of western Europe that had fought in two recent wars, to then become, half a century later, a peace pact between countries that had fought in the subsequent Cold War. Economic growth was considered a condition for the promotion of peace, welfare, and freedom rather than an end in itself. Of course, if with the Treaties of Rome of 1957 the conditions were created for an *economic* pact among former enemies, the institution of NATO in 1949 (in turn strengthened in 1955 with the adhesion of the Federal Republic of Germany) created the conditions for a *military* pact among them, a pact guaranteed by the predominant presence of the US in that organization (Calleo 2001). The institutional disconnection between the economic and the military pact has inevitably affected the path and intensity of the integration's process. As Riker (1975: 114) argued, "In every successful formed federalism it must be the case that a significant external or internal threat or a significant opportunity for aggression is present, where the threat can be forestalled and the aggression carried out only with a bigger government." Although Riker did not distinguish between types of federation, the external threat's argument is true for the federal aggregation of previously independent states (and not for the federal disaggregation of a previously unitary state). Indeed, Riker (1975: 114) observed that the threat's neutralization constitutes "the main feature, the prospective gain, in both giving and accepting the bargain [for creating a union]." In the EU case, after the failure of the 1954 ECD project, that threat was dealt with through NATO. Consequently, the federal aim was reinterpreted in economic terms, i.e., the building of a common market became the instrument for advancing toward an "ever closer union among the peoples of Europe" (as the 1957 Rome Treaties' Preamble declared). Market-making came to be a process excessively overloaded in political terms (Scharpf 2016).

After all, the Westphalian system of nation states (Westphalian because it emerged from the Peace of Westphalia of 1648, a peace that ended a long sequence of wars through the formation of homogeneous political entities, the states, marked by the control of an authority over the population of a given territory), which the Europeans had invented, had proven anything but capable of guaranteeing peace on the continent through the balance of power. Indeed, that system had been the source of permanent insecurity, thus activating periodic attempts, on the part of one or another European nation state, to impose its imperial order on the continent. Thus, after two wars between Europeans that became global conflicts, the European nation states (starting with the continental nation states) had to acknowledge that they would have no future unless they created a new political order. The threat represented by the Cold War and the presence of the US on the continent (which, as a non-European power, was seen as a guarantee by European countries; Ikenberry 2000) was a further reason to start the integration process. The EU is therefore the outcome of an attempt to escape from the Westphalian solution of interstate rivalries, even if this attempt could not receive (after the ECD's defeat) a political justification to match its historical importance. The need to provide a constitutional justification for the European integration process emerged only with the end of the Cold War.

With the EU, European nation states contributed to creating a supranational order aimed at facilitating increasingly close economic cooperation among them, on issues of common interest through the interaction between intergovernmental and supranational (frequently called "community") institutions. As history had amply demonstrated, not only political peace but also economic growth could not be achieved only through strictly international (or interstate) agreements. Those agreements, in order to be respected, required the existence of institutions independent from the national governments that had created them, and thus put in a position to regulate the rivalries that were destined to emerge among those national governments. The task assigned to the European Commission and to the European Court of Justice, therefore, consisted of guaranteeing that the signatories to the intergovernmental agreements complied with the rules that they had set themselves. Thus, the supranational component of the EU (the

Commission and the European Court of Justice and then, increasingly, the European Parliament) was necessary to protect the interstate component (represented originally by the Council of Ministers) from the possible fallout of rivalries among the states. In this sense, the EU is an attempt to domesticate the external relations of the European nation states, creating a supranational regime with domestic characteristics.

The material bases of the peace pact were represented by transnational cooperation on an increasing number of economic issues (Lindberg 1963). This cooperation led to the gradual institutionalization of a complex network of bodies, some envisaged by the founding treaties (such as the Council of Ministers, the Commission, and the European Parliament) and others not (such as the European Council). Thus, between the 1960s and the 1980s, a system was institutionalized that was not comparable to an international organization, even if it could not be considered a domestic organization. The institution that had originally been preeminent, the Council of Ministers, had to recognize the considerable influence that the Commission could exercise in the policy-making process, thanks to its monopoly of power in initiating legislative proposals (also justified by its acknowledged technical skills). In addition, it has to recognize the growth of the decision-making role of the European Parliament, which, starting with its direct elections in 1979, had successfully claimed power, first to co-determine and then to co-decide in an increasingly broad range of policies (a power recognized since the Single European Act of 1986). This was a significant increase of power for an institution originally named (in the 1957 Rome Treaties) as a European parliamentary assembly (and which became the European Parliament in 1962) and constituted, until 1979, by delegates of national parliaments. Then all three institutions had to recognize the strategic role of the European Council of heads of government, which became (as of its first informal meetings in 1974) the arena in which to define the EU's long-term choices or to solve interstate tensions. Naturally, the political driver of the integration process had continued to be the so-called Franco-German axis, which set the time frames and the direction of the integration process (Hendricks and Morgan 2001).

In short, between the 1960s and the 1980s, the EU was institutionalized through interaction between supranational and intergovernmental institutions, interaction that was then termed the community or supranational method (Dehousse 2011) by one of the inspirers of the European integration process, Jean Monnet (Duchene 1994). The supranational or community side and the intergovernmental side continued to grow together, in a way that was simultaneously competitive and cooperative. Right from its foundation in 1957, the EU has passed through a process of institutional development that has significantly transformed its original nature of an organization legitimated by interstate treaties (Stone Sweet, Sandholtz, and Fligstein 2001). This development institutionalized a quite complex but sufficiently stable collection of bodies that came to share the decision-making responsibility in a growing number of public policies (a system here defined as supranational). In this process, the European Court of Justice had a crucial role, introducing constitutional criteria in the operation of the supranational system and in its dealings with the states participating in the integration process (Kelemen 2011). Consider the two crucial decisions of the 1960s: one which established, in *Van Gend en Loos* of 1962, that certain community provisions have a direct effect on individual citizens and not only on the governments of the member states; and the other which established, in *Costa vs Enel* of 1964, that in the case of conflict between community legislation and the legislation of the member states, the former has priority over the latter, even if the latter was approved subsequently. These decisions helped create a genuine supranational order – in other words, to constitutionalize the operation of the common market (Amato and Ziller 2007). At the end of the 1980s, the European nation states had been fully transformed into member states of the EU (Sbragia 1994), a transformation become irreversible in the following decades (Bickerton 2012).

From Maastricht to Lisbon

In the initial decades, the integration process took place in western Europe, it could benefit from the political cover and military protection of the US (through their leadership of NATO), and it was based on the division of Germany (which had been the unresolved European problem at least since the Franco-Prussian War of 1871, with its dramatic outcome of the coronation of the Prussian emperor in the palace of Versailles). Between 1989 and 1991, these systemic conditions of integration weakened irremediably. With the fall of the Berlin Wall in November 1989, the problem of German unification came to the fore and, with the implosion of the Soviet Union in August 1991, the end of the Cold War became a reality. Integrated Europe was forced to change its agenda. The EU could no longer limit itself to creating a single market, leaving to others (i.e., the US) the task of guaranteeing its military security. And above all, it could no longer think that the reunification of Germany could be deferred indefinitely. Indeed, such reunification happened at the end (October) of 1990, with the help of the Americans and the doubts of the main European governments, but in exchange for the Germans giving up their national currency (the *Deutsche Mark*) and supporting the formation of an Economic and Monetary Union (EMU, hereafter known as the Eurozone) to manage a new common currency (the euro). The Treaty of Maastricht of 1992, which was drafted by the previous year's intergovernmental conference, was the European response to these historic changes.

After the 1954 defeat of the EDC's project, for the first time, in preparing the treaty, it was recognized that the integration project should have a political and not a solely economic nature. For the first time, there was talk of *political union*, to the extent that the name "European Union" would be introduced to mark the distance from the previous name "European Economic Community." For the first time, it was decided that the integration process should involve policy sectors not strictly connected to the single market (as formalized by the Single European Act of 1986), such as foreign and security policy and justice and home affairs policy. For the first time, the time frames and the means were defined to adopt a common currency that could contain the economic force of Germany. However, these acknowledgments could not cancel the divergences between states. Thus, at the Intergovernmental Conference two fundamental compromises were signed. The first was the compromise between the states in favor of political integration and the states that were interested only in constructing a single market. The states interested in political union were authorized to go ahead, allowing others to rule themselves out (through the so-called opt-out clause) from the more integrated policies (such as that of the common currency). The second compromise was celebrated in the group of states in favor of political integration, between those that wanted to follow the path of constructing an entirely supranational union and those instead that wanted to strengthen the control of national governments over new policies (those traditionally close to core state powers) (Fabbrini 2015a).

The result was a treaty based on three pillars: the supranational pillar of the single market (called the European Communities) and the two intergovernmental pillars of the Common Foreign and Security Policy

(CFSP) and the Justice and Home Affairs (JHA) policy. This treaty formally recognized that the EU could proceed in the integration process in crucial areas for its member states provided that their governments were guaranteed an exclusive decision-making role thanks to the strengthening of the intergovernmental institutions. This idea of *differentiating the decision-making regimes* further consolidated with the start of the Eurozone in 1994. In order to respond to the German problem, it was decided that there would be the creation of a new (common) currency, the euro, managed by a genuinely federal institution, the European Central Bank, designed on the basis of the institutional model of the German federal bank, the *Deutsche Bundesbank*, provided that the states maintained their freedom of action in policies linked to the common currency (such as fiscal and budgetary policy and, more generally, economic policy). However, this freedom of action, which was requested by the French government (James 2012; Tuori and Tuori 2014), was limited by the statutory definition of restrictions regarding the levels of deficit and public debt within which the economic policy of the individual states belonging to the Eurozone could be undertaken. This limitation was imposed by the German government, worried that there might be a situation of moral hazard, by which some states could transfer the cost of their choices (or non-choices) to other states. Thus in 1997–1998, the Stability and Growth Pact was formalized, consisting of a resolution and two regulations. With the latter, the Council of Ministers of July 1997 decided to set the parameters within which the voluntary coordination should be undertaken. The first regulation (which came into force on July 1, 1998) intervened upstream, because it established the procedure for the surveillance of public budgets and for the coordination of the national economic policies. The second regulation (which came into force on January 1, 1999) intervened downstream, because it established the implementation procedure to be activated in the case of excessive deficit. The combination of these two regulations formed the Stability and Growth Pact, then recognized in the subsequent treaties. These regulations, once approved, had to be applied as they were by the member states.

The decision made in 1994 was therefore coherent with the system established in Maastricht: centralizing monetary policy and decentralizing the economic (budgetary and fiscal) policies connected to it. The integration progressed to the point of calling into question one of the pillars of the modern state, monetary sovereignty, but the member states and their governments had set in place an institutional model that entrusted them with control over the decision-making process relating to the connected fiscal and budgetary policies, more generally to those policies that the end of the Cold War had pushed on to the European agenda (Dyson 2012). After three stages of convergence, the euro thus came into circulation on January 1, 2002, becoming (at the time of this writing) the common currency of nineteen (initially eleven) of the member states of the EU (Austria, Belgium, Cyprus, Estonia, Finland, France, Germany, Greece, Ireland, Italy, Latvia, Lithuania, Luxembourg, Malta, the Netherlands, Portugal, Slovakia, Slovenia, Spain).

During the 1990s, the need to accommodate within the EU the new countries of eastern and southern Europe had ended up keeping open the so-called institutional building site. In that decade, a sequence of treaties was approved that, in turn, joined those that had given birth to the integration process: the Rome Treaties (1957), the Single European Act (1986), the Treaty of Maastricht (1992), the Treaty of Amsterdam (1997), and the Treaty of Nice (2001). Given the prospect of a doubling of the number of member states, it was then decided to move toward a rationalization of this complex structure of treaties to enable the EU to operate with greater legitimacy and effectiveness. In 2002–2003, a Constitutional Convention was called in Brussels that drafted a new text, the Constitutional Treaty (formally, the "Treaty establishing a Constitution for Europe"), which had to replace all the other treaties (Norman 2003). Although signed by the heads of state and government in a solemn meeting held in Rome in October 2004, the Constitutional Treaty was then blocked by French and Dutch voters in two referenda held in May and June 2005, respectively. After some reflection, it was decided to amend the existing treaties, incorporating much of the Constitutional Treaty in a new text called the Lisbon Treaty (because it was signed in the Portuguese capital). The Irish voted against the Lisbon Treaty in June 2008 but were then convinced to support that treaty in a subsequent referendum held in October 2009. The Lisbon Treaty came into force on December 1, 2009.

The Lisbon Treaty formally consists of three treaties: the Treaty of Maastricht on the European Union of 1992 as amended (Treaty on the European Union, or TEU) and the Treaties of Rome of 1957 as amended (and renamed the Treaty on the Functioning of the European Union, or TFEU), plus the Charter of Fundamental Rights (the existence of which was acknowledged by the Intergovernmental Conference that drafted the Treaty of Nice of 2001 but that had not then formalized it). The sequence of the treaties (see Table 1.1) bears witness to the complex process of institutionalizing the EU. The Lisbon Treaty seemed to represent the conclusion of that process. Things, however, did not turn out as many had expected. The multiple crises of the post-Lisbon period have in fact reopened the institutional building site.

The Lisbon Treaty: The Supranational Constitution

If the Lisbon Treaty abolished the division into pillars formalized at Maastricht, nonetheless it preserved the distinction between different decision-making regimes in relation to different European policies. It can be said that the Lisbon Treaty formalized a dual decision-making system, or, better, a dual constitution (Fabbrini 2015a). It institutionalized a *supranational constitution* to regulate policies connected to the single market having a low domestic political salience. At the same time, it institutionalized an *intergovernmental constitution* to regulate policies that are sensitive for member states because of their high domestic political salience. In the former case, an institutional quadrilateral was formalized, based on a bicameral legislative arm (the Council of Ministers, because it is the chamber that represents governments in the form of sectorial ministers, and the European Parliament, because it is the chamber representing citizens) and a dual executive (the European Commission, with a commissioner for each member state, and the European Council, consisting of the heads of government of member states).

This quadrilateral has the features of a quasi-separation of powers system of government (Hix and Hoyland 2011: ch. 2). In single market policies, the Commission and its president (owing both to the prerogatives and the technical competences that they have available) are more important than the European Council. Albeit the European Council has been recognized to have an executive role, this concerns the definition of the EU's long-term strategies. The European Council is no longer (as it was before the Lisbon Treaty) the highest form of the Council of Ministers, but, in this constitution, it does not have a strictly decision-making role. It is a kind of collegial "head of state" of the EU, the last-resort umpire for unsolvable disputes that may emerge within the EU. The legislative co–decision-making of the Council of Ministers

Table 1.1 *Treaties of the European Union*

Treaties	Member states	Purposes
European Coal and Steel Community ECSC (Paris, 1951)	Belgium, France, Germany, Italy, Luxembourg, the Netherlands	Guarantee equal access of the member states to the coal and steel market
EURATOM (Rome 1957)	Belgium, France, Germany, Italy, Luxembourg, the Netherlands	Promote nuclear research and technology in the member states
European Economic Community EEC (Rome, 1957)	Belgium, France, Germany, Italy, Luxembourg, the Netherlands	Create a common market among the member states
Single European Act SEA (Luxembourg, 1986)	Denmark, Belgium, France, Germany, Ireland, Italy, Luxembourg, the Netherlands, the United Kingdom	Launch a single market among the member states
European Union EU (Maastricht, 1992)	Denmark, Belgium, France, Germany, Ireland, Italy, Luxembourg, the Netherlands, the United Kingdom	Organization with three pillars: • Supranational pillar for the single market • Intergovernmental pillar for foreign and security policy • Intergovernmental pillar for justice and home affairs policy • Decision to create an economic and monetary union (Eurozone)
European Community EC (Amsterdam, 1997)	Austria, Denmark, Belgium, Finland, Greece, Germany, Ireland, Italy,	Reorganization of the first pillar in a new treaty (EC)

Table 1.1 (*cont.*)

Treaties	Member states	Purposes
	Luxembourg, the Netherlands, Sweden, the United Kingdom	
Nice (2001)	Austria, Denmark, Belgium, Finland, Greece, Germany, Ireland, Italy, Luxembourg, the Netherlands, Sweden, the United Kingdom	Acknowledgment of the Charter of Fundamental Rights Rationalization of the institutional system
Lisbon Treaty (2009)	Austria, Belgium, Bulgaria, Czech Republic, Denmark, Cyprus, Estonia, Finland, France, Germany, Greece, Hungary, Ireland, Italy, Latvia, Lithuania, Luxembourg, Malta, the Netherlands, Poland, Portugal, Romania, Slovakia, Slovenia, Spain, Sweden, the United Kingdom, Croatia (2013)	Abolition of the pillars but dual decision-making regime: supranational and intergovernmental Formal recognition of the Charter of Fundamental Rights Attribution of legal personality to the EU

(a functional legislative body chaired by a rotating national minister on a biannual basis) and the European Parliament is established as the ordinary procedure by which to approve European laws (regulations and directives), while the Commission maintains the power to start the legislative process (putting a particular proposal of regulation or directive to one or the other of the two chambers) and the European Council sees its role recognized as the strategic head of the EU executive (with the duty of defining the EU's strategies, as well as resolving interstate conflicts that could block the functioning of the latter). It is a supranational system of government because the roles and functions of the various institutions are sufficiently specified. It is a quasi-separate system of government because no institution depends on the political confidence of the others to function as such.

Certainly, with the choice of the so-called *Spitzenkandidaten*, the parties of the European Parliament sought to free the election of the president of the Commission from the control of the European Council (Christiansen 2016). According to TEU Article 17.7, indeed, "Taking into account the elections to the European Parliament and after having held the appropriate consultations, the European Council, acting by a qualified majority, shall propose to the European Parliament a candidate for President of the Commission. This candidate shall be elected by the European Parliament by a majority of its component members. If he does not obtain the required majority, the European Council, acting by a qualified majority, shall within one month propose a new candidate who shall be elected by the European Parliament following the same procedure." In the elections for the European Parliament of May 2014, the biggest European parties identified a "top candidate" as the possible president of the Commission, should (obviously) one or another of them win the relative majority (plurality) of the votes for the election of the European parliamentarians. The European People's Party, which had indicated the Luxembourg politician Jean-Claude Juncker as its *Spitzenkandidat*, in obtaining the greatest number of seats in those elections, therefore proposed the latter as president of the Commission. This proposal was accompanied by the warning to the European Council, from the main parties in the European Parliament, that the latter would not vote for any other candidate as president of the Commission. Because the vote of the European Parliament is necessary to confirm the choice of the European Council, the warning had the desired effect. The European Council indicated Juncker as candidate to the presidency of the Commission, then putting that name to the European Parliament.

However, that of the European Council was only a partial surrender. Indeed, the choice of the other twenty-seven members of the Commission did not follow the electoral logic used for the president of the Commission. The commissioners were suggested by the European Council (albeit consulting the newly elected president of the Commission) for voting by the European Parliament on the basis of national more than party considerations. Unlike in the past, the majority of commissioners had previously held key positions in their respective national governments. Of the twenty-seven commissioners appointed, five had been prime ministers, two deputy prime ministers, one a secretary of state, three European parliamentarians, one the leader of the conservatives in the House of Lords, and six were previous European commissioners. Many spoke of it as being a quasi-intergovernmental Commission. Although there was uneasiness on the part of national leaders with this practice, the Commission (in its Communication of February 13, 2018, p. 4) argued that the *Spitzenkandidat* or "lead candidate system had a positive impact on the relationship between the EU institutions and thus on the efficiency of the work of all of them," thus asserting that "the experiment of 2014 should continue." Indeed, according to the Commission, "going one step further would be to have the President of the European Commission directly elected by citizens. (...) However, this would require a change in the Treaties."

Even if the Commission and its president are proposed by the European Council and then elected by the European Parliament, they cannot be compared to a parliamentary government (Fabbrini 2015b). The European Parliament can dismiss the Commission only on the grounds of not respecting governmental ethics (it did that in 1999; Moury 2007), not on the grounds of political disagreement, nor can the Commission dissolve the European Parliament, because the latter has a five-year mandate established by the treaty. In short, there is no relationship of reciprocal political confidence between the parliamentary majority and the Commission. The institutions are reciprocally independent and at the same time connected to each other through a mechanism of checks and balances. In this constitution, the European Parliament has acquired equal legislative standing with the Council of Ministers, motivating wisely and doggedly its requests for institutional influence with the fact of being the only institution directly elected (since 1979) by the citizens of the individual member states of the EU (Rittberger 2003). The increased influence of the European Parliament has, however, reduced the Commission's role of establishing the agenda as the supranational institution par excellence (Kreppel and Oztas 2016). At the same time, the European Parliament, by imposing co–decision-making as the ordinary procedure of the EU in single market policies, has given legitimacy to the legislative process, removing it from the behind-closed-doors machinations of the past.

Therefore, in all the policies linked to the single market, the EU continues to operate through the approval of legislative provisions (regulations and directives), an activity that is rigorously monitored by the European Court of Justice. It is this *integration through law* that is at the origin of the integration process and that is guaranteed by a complex political and legal system that can satisfy the basic criteria for the effectiveness and legitimacy of decisions (Craig 2011). In particular with the Lisbon Treaty, which strengthened the role of the European Parliament and institutionalized the complex system of checks and balances, the supranational EU has acquired a satisfactory democratic form. Moreover, the European Court of Justice has seen its role ensured as guarantor (if not promoter) of integration through law, acting as the institution with the role of resolving disputes between member states and EU institutions, as well as between the latter themselves. The role of the European Court of Justice has been fundamental in promoting the formation of the single market (Stone Sweet 2000). With the Lisbon Treaty, the system of supranational government became sufficiently stable to be able to investigate the regularity of its operation. It formalizes an institutional architecture that is based on a distinction between legislative and executive institutions, as in democratic systems of government. Yet, this institutional architecture regulates the policy making of issues with limited domestic political salience.

The Lisbon Treaty: The Intergovernmental Constitution

The Lisbon Treaty also constitutionalized an intergovernmental decision-making regime. At Maastricht, this regime had received specific formalization in ad hoc pillars. With the Lisbon Treaty, the division into pillars was abolished, but the differentiation between different decision-making regimes remained. With the extension of integration to crucial policy areas for member states (because of their high domestic political salience), governments placed those areas in an institutional context very different compared with that regulating the numerous policies linked to the single market. Thus, even if the Lisbon Treaty was an innovation compared with the Treaty of Maastricht, nonetheless it institutionalized differentiated decision-making regimes, on the one hand, for single market policies and, on the other, for Common Foreign and Security Policy (CFSP), Justice and Home Affairs (JHA) policy, and economic policy for the Eurozone, inter alia. For the latter, the Lisbon Treaty suspended the aforementioned decision-making quadrilateral to replace it with an institutional arrangement based mainly on the European Council of heads of government and the Council of Ministers of the member states. In relation to these latter policies, the purpose indicated by the Lisbon Treaty is that of facilitating the coordination of the policies of member states, but not their legal integration at the supranational level. The decisions must be made through specific means, sometimes defined as a new mode of governance (Heritier and Rhodes 2010) and sometimes as deliberative intergovernmentalism (Puetter 2012).

Let us start with foreign and security policy (CFSP). TEU Art. 24.1 is explicit in stating that "the adoption of legislative acts shall be excluded." Albeit strengthening the Amsterdam Treaty's innovation of a High Representative for foreign and security policy who is the permanent president (for five years) of the Foreign Affairs Council consisting of the corresponding ministers of the member states (the only formation of the Council outside of the half-year presidency system) and who is at the same time the vice president of the Commission, the Lisbon Treaty did not change the intergovernmental logic established by the Treaty of Maastricht for foreign policy (Amadio Viceré 2018). The coordination must take place (TEU Art. 25) through decisions consisting of "actions and positions," which, once adopted, the member states *voluntarily* undertake to respect. In this decision-making regime, the Commission, through its vice president, must act as technical support to the Foreign Affairs Council, but may not exercise any political role (which is the responsibility of the European Council). At the same time, the European Parliament must be consulted, but it is not allowed to exercise any checking and balancing role on the intergovernmental institutions. And because the common foreign and security policy is made through political decisions, and not legislative acts, the European Court of Justice is precluded from exercising significant judicial supervision.

This is also true for the EU's economic policy. The decisions are the responsibility solely of the Council of Economic and Finance Ministers (known as the ECOFIN Council), which may recommend the adoption of corrective measures by a member state, even if TEU Art. 126.6 gives the Commission the role of activating the procedures for excessive budget deficits on the part of a member state. In any case, the

Commission may make a *proposal*, but it is again the responsibility of the ECOFIN Council to decide whether to proceed or not in conformity with the Commission's proposal. This is even more true for the measures that concern member states of the Eurozone, where the decision-making role of the Eurogroup is institutionalized (Puetter 2006). This is the group of finance ministers from the Eurozone, led by a permanent president for five years (elected by the other ministers and accountable to them). The economic policy enshrined by the Lisbon Treaty is based mainly on measures of voluntary coordination among the member states. The result is that the Lisbon Treaty has centralized, with the euro, the management of the common currency (through the supranational role of the European Central Bank) and at the same time has decentralized to the states of the Eurozone all the (fiscal and budgetary) policies connected to the common currency. Both the Stability and Growth Pact (which covers all the member states) and the measures relating to the euro are decided by the ECOFIN Council (and therefore by the finance ministers of the Eurozone meeting in the Eurogroup), with a technical support role for the Commission, a very marginal controlling role for the European Parliament, and limited judicial supervision by the European Court of Justice.

With the deepening of the integration process, there has been constant growth in the role of governments (through the European Council). The European Council has gradually distanced itself from the Council of Ministers, taking on a purely executive function (that of establishing the broad brushstrokes of EU policy), leaving to the Council of Ministers the role of the chamber of the states, as in a federal legislative system. The growth of the role of the European Council has led to a downsizing of the role of the Council of Ministers as the intergovernmental institution par excellence. Moreover, the election (with the Lisbon Treaty) of a permanent president of the European Council, who is elected for two and a half years with a renewable mandate for a second term of similar length, has institutionalized its decision-making power, providing continuity to its executive action. Just consider that if the Lisbon Treaty envisages that it "meets twice every six months" (TEU Art. 15.3), with the multiple crises that have taken place in the post-Lisbon period and with the growth in importance in the European agenda of strategic policies, the European Council has ended up meeting on a much more regular basis (between 2010 and 2017, on average seven meetings each year, to which must be added the equally frequent meetings of the heads of government of the countries of the Eurozone). During the financial and migration crises or the security crisis, the Commission was not the driving force of the integration process, even if it was clear that its technical skills were essential for translating the decisions made by the European Council into operational measures (Puetter 2014).

In short, as early as the Treaty of Maastricht of 1992 it was formally established that the EU's economic and financial policy be defined and regulated within an intergovernmental decision-making regime. With the rejection of the Constitutional Treaty in the referenda held in France and the Netherlands in 2005, the intergovernmental logic seemed to be the anchor for the more general integration process. The latter, particularly in the most politically salient policies, could proceed only through the lead of national governments, organized in the European Council of heads of government of the member states of the EU and finally coordinated by a permanent president, as well as represented by their ministers on the various functional councils. Indeed, seeing that the force of history had led the EU to handle policies traditionally at the heart of the national sovereignty of member states (and electorally sensitive for the fates of their incumbent governments), no one questioned the decision to promote, in those policies, an integration model based on the voluntary coordination of national policies – in other words, a model necessarily without any legal restrictions on member state choices (Bickerton, Hodson, and Puetter 2015).

This is why it is possible to argue that the Lisbon Treaty has institutionalized a dual constitutional regime (although combinations of the two regimes continue to take place in specific micro- or sub-policy issues, Heritier 2007). Regarding the management of public policies linked to the single market, the Lisbon Treaty envisaged a supranational constitutional model. This constitution supports and justifies a decision-making system marked by a separation of powers (albeit informal) among the four institutions that participate in the policy-making process (a dual executive consisting of the European Council and the Commission and a bicameral legislative body consisting of the European Parliament and the Council of Ministers). At the same time, regarding the policies that are traditionally sensitive for national sovereignty, the Lisbon Treaty institutionalized an intergovernmental constitutional model based, first of all, on the centralization of decision-making in the two institutions (the European Council and the Council of Ministers) that represent the governments of the member states of the EU and then, second, on a confusion of powers, as is the case, for example, of the Foreign Affairs Council or the ECOFIN Council, at the same time both legislative and executive institutions.

If it is possible to argue that the supranational constitutional model justifies a system of government marked by a division of powers (albeit contradictory) among the four institutions that participate in the decision-making process, the intergovernmental governance's model has instead come to be based on the centralization of decision-making in the European Council and the Council of Ministers according to a logic of confusion of powers. Regarding the intergovernmental regime, consider the following aspects: The ECOFIN Council and the Eurogroup are legislative institutions that, nonetheless, have executive functions. This is also true for the (five-year) president of the Eurogroup, who carries out both legislative and executive functions. At the same time, the High Representative for Foreign and Security Policy is the vice president of the Commission (an executive body) and president (for five years) of the Foreign Affairs Council (a formation of the Council of Ministers, theoretically a legislative body). Moreover, the Commission, although it is an executive body, is not institutionally linked to the European Council, which is an executive institution. The European Council's works are prepared by the General Secretariat of the Council of Ministers, an institution that is, in turn, legislative. The Council of Ministers (which is primarily a legislative institution) and the European Council (which is primarily an executive institution) continue to overlap in operational terms through the General Secretariat of the Council of Ministers. The intergovernmental constitution unlikely satisfies the criterion of democratic legitimacy. Indeed, if we use the analytical criteria with which empirical democracies are assessed, it is not possible to consider as legitimate a decision made by the European Council, in its executive role, bereft of checks and balances (at the level where it is made) by the European Parliament, unless one assumes that a collegial decision of the European Council is legitimate because the single members of that institution enjoy the distinct legitimacy of their national parliaments. In the intergovernmental constitution, the European Parliament has no power to sanction the choices of the European Council, choices that are supposed to be checked by national parliaments (Neyer 2015), an unrealistic supposition. Moreover, in the case of decisions made by the Euro Summit or Eurogroup, the European

Parliament cannot distinguish internally between representatives elected in countries of the Eurozone and representatives elected in countries that are not part of the Eurozone. Because the European Parliament represents, with the Lisbon Treaty, the citizens of the EU, and no longer the citizens of the single member states of the EU, as was the case with the Maastricht Treaty, this has inevitably complicated its internal differentiation.

The institutional confusion of the intergovernmental constitution has already generated dramatic implications at the national level. The decision-making monopoly of the intergovernmental institutions has encouraged a process of centralization that has ended up blurring the distinction between the national and the European levels. In this way, the battery of the subsidiarity clause has been exhausted, i.e., there has remained no possibility for member state parliaments to question the choices made by the intergovernmental institutions of Brussels. If the decisions in Brussels are made by bodies also consisting of their prime minister or minister, then it is unthinkable that a national parliament (whose majority is expressed in that prime minister or minister) can call into question the decisions made. Moreover, having no firewalls between the national and the European levels, the inter-governmental constitution makes it possible for a national cough to be transformed into a European Council bronchitis. One has only to think of what might happen if anti-EU leaders, winning national elections, come to constitute a majority within the European Council. Under the pressure of events, national governments, coordinating through and within the European Council and Council of Ministers, have taken control of the decision-making process, seeking solutions regularly challenged owing to their ineffectiveness (because the unanimity's criteria does not help in reaching decisions in difficult times) and illegitimacy (because each member of the European Council or the Euro Summit is answerable to their own national parliament, and yet the institutions deliver European and not national decisions). Facing crises with interstate distributive effects, the political role of the European Council has become convoluted. Its collegiality was suspended by a hierarchical logic, with the governments of the larger and stronger member states imposing their agenda on the other governments (Fabbrini, 2016a).

In sum, the supranational governance's model has guaranteed a certain balance between the intergovernmental and supranational institutions, but in policies with limited domestic political impact. The intergovernmental governance's model, having assigned the decisions on policies with high domestic political impact to the European Council, assumed to be controlled by national parliaments, has ended up not only reducing the role of supranational institutions such as the Commission and the European Parliament but also obscuring the distinction between national and European politics.

Conclusion

The Lisbon Treaty represents the outcome of a long and controversial process of public discussion on the constitutional identity of the EU. This chapter has shown that, contrary to a processual view, the EU has come to institutionalize a highly structured, although internally differentiated, decision-making process. With the 1992 Treaty of Maastricht, European integration had already started to involve areas of public policies that were considered the core of national sovereignty. After Maastricht, not only did the policy areas linked to the single market expand, but also the high-policy areas for the individual member states (such as foreign and security policy, justice and home affairs policy, and finally economic policy) entered the EU (as opposed to the national) agenda. The regional integration process was becoming so deep (as well as so extended, with the subsequent enlargements) that it inevitably required a greater definition of its institutional arrangements and decision-making procedures. The Lisbon Treaty, abolishing the division into pillars but keeping the difference in the decision-making regimes, institutionalized a decision-making differentiation that started with the Maastricht Treaty. It institutionalized a supranational regime to regulate policies connected to the single market and, at the same time, an intergovernmental system to manage policies strategic for the member states and electorally sensitive for their governmental leaders. In the first case, it is a system of quasi separation of powers, because no institution depends on the political confidence of the others in order to be able to function as such, even if with the *Spitzenkandidat* the political affinity has increased between the majority in the European Parliament and the Commission. In any case, the role and functions of the institutions are distinct and specified. In the second case, it is a system of confusion of powers, because the decisions are made by the national governments (through the European Council, which coordinates them) or by their ministers (operationally aggregated in the Councils of Ministers managing intergovernmental policies, as the ECOFIN Council and Foreign Affairs Council), which behave as both executive and legislative institutions. Moreover, those institutions operate largely unchecked by the supranational institutions. In strategic policies, not only is the Commission no longer the driving force of the integration process, even if its technical competences continue to be indispensable to translate the decisions made by the European Council into operational measures, but above all the European Parliament is playing a subordinate role. Thus, while the supranational constitution has led to a strengthening of the European Parliament, which has imposed co–decision-making as the ordinary procedure of the EU, the intergovernmental constitution has led to the strengthening of the European Council, which has imposed its political, and not only strategic, centrality. Paradoxically, the two institutions that emerged as the most influential from the process of institutionalization, the European Parliament (in the supranational constitution) and the European Council (in the intergovernmental constitution), in the 1957 Rome Treaties were either not set up (the latter) or consisted of representatives of the national parliaments with exclusively consultative power (the former).

The supranational constitution has guaranteed a certain balance between institutions, but in policies with limited domestic political impact. For this reason, that constitution has not assigned a decision-making role to the European Council, but instead assigned it the function of being the ultimate arbiter for disagreements between states (a kind of crisis manager). In turn, the intergovernmental constitution, based on the intermingling between national and European levels of government, has ended up reducing the role of supranational institutions such as the Commission and the European Parliament, to the point of creating a system of (horizontal and vertical) confusion of powers. With the Lisbon Treaty, therefore, two principles or approaches to the integration process were institutionalized. There is integration through the law that celebrates the role of the European Court of Justice as the institution entrusted with the task not only of overseeing the legislative process, but also of resolving legal disputes between member states and EU institutions as well as among the latter. At the same time, with the extension of integration to politically crucial policy areas for member states, governments have placed the new policies in decision-making environments that are quite different from those that govern regulatory policies of the single market. Here, it is integration through the voluntary coordination of policies by national governments, coordination that takes place within the European Council and the functional Council of Ministers. In relation to these policies, the purpose indicated is that of facilitating the consensual management of crucial policies for the member states, but not their legal integration at the supranational level. Even if the Lisbon Treaty ended the division into pillars established by the 1992 Treaty of Maastricht, it institutionalized legal frameworks and decision-making regimes that were different for single market and strategic policies. This dual approach to integration may help in understanding why the multiple crises of the post-Lisbon era, because they fell to the intergovernmental constitution, did not lead to a supranationalization of the integration process, as expected by many and conceptualized by Jean Monnet some time ago. We will now turn our attention to these crises for better understanding the consequences of the intergovernmental constitution.

2 | *Intergovernmental Governance and Its Implications*

Introduction

The EU has changed radically during the multiple crises of the 2010s. Those crises have called into question the balance between the two constitutions envisaged by the Lisbon Treaty, impetuously strengthening the intergovernmental constitution to which the treaty entrusted the management of economic, migration, and security policies. When the crises exploded, the EU had available the decision-making framework to handle them, within which to identify the instruments necessary to regulate those crises (and to prevent others). For this reason, it is unfair to argue that the EU was unprepared to address the challenges of the euro crisis or the migration crisis. However, it is also clear that the instruments the EU had available did not work as expected. The euro crisis continued in a manner never seen in other such currency crises. The decisions made were often too limited (compared with what was necessary) and always arrived too late (compared with the very quick time frames for the choices made by the finance markets). The difficulty in managing the euro crisis increased the divisions within the Eurozone between the debtor states of the south and the creditor states of the north. This division was epitomized by the asymmetric effects of the euro crisis, with the southern member states of the Eurozone paying a much higher cost than the northern member states.

In a context in which the prolonged euro crisis had structurally weakened political cohesion within the EU and social cohesion within its member states, the arrival in Europe of huge waves of political refugees and economic migrants added fuel to the fire. On the basis of the agreements, albeit revised, which led to the Dublin Convention, the management of immigration was left to individual countries, specifically those where the migrants had first arrived in the EU. Political and economic migration quickly became the main concern of national governments and public opinion, particularly of the southern states where the migration's influx arrived more easily. In conjunction with the terrorist attacks, migration ended up summarizing all the negative or threatening aspects of the European integration process, as well as of the process of globalization. Whether alleged or real, the threat of the invasion of Europe by non-European populations from the poorer areas of Africa or areas devastated by the war in the Middle East provided a tremendous opportunity for populist leaders and movements to mobilize citizens' fears. In the case of security policy, the EU mainly used the instruments of intergovernmental coordination, as they were defined in the second and third pillars of the Treaty of Maastricht of 1992. It is striking that the multiple crises occurred in those policy areas that national governments had wanted to keep under their close control. It is also striking that the crises remained unresolved owing to the difficulty of addressing them through the logic of voluntary coordination. Finally, Brexit caused centrifugal Europe to take a stride forward (Zielonka 2014), although secession has not become the alternative to integration. This chapter investigates why the intergovernmental constitution has not worked as expected. It is organized as follows: First, it conceptualizes the main dilemmas of the intergovernmental constitution. Second, it analyzes the intergovernmental management of the euro crisis. Third, it analyzes the migration crisis and its security implications. Finally, it discusses the political consequences, at the domestic level, of the intergovernmental governance of policies of strategic importance for the member states.

Dilemmas of the Intergovernmental Constitution

The financial crisis represented (in institutional terms) a formidable test of the governance capabilities of the intergovernmental constitution. The test returned a broadly unsatisfactory result. As envisaged by the Lisbon Treaty, the European Council was the real decision-making center for the policies created to respond to the euro crisis, with the Commission limited to exercising a technical support role or a role of implementing decisions made by national leaders or finance ministers within the ECOFIN Council. The intergovernmental constitution did not manage to satisfactorily resolve three basic dilemmas of the integration process: the dilemma of the power of veto, the dilemma of respect of the agreements, and the dilemma of the legitimacy of the decisions. Let us see why (Fabbrini 2013).

If integration is based on coordination among national policies, i.e., on the principle of unanimity in decisions, then it is no surprise that every decision (to respond to the euro crisis) took a lot of time. After all, within the European Council there were heads of government who represented different economic interests, those of the creditor states of northern Europe and those of the debtor states of the south, just as within the European Council itself different strategies of economic governance vied with each other (such as the ordo-liberal monetarism of Germany and the Colbertian neo-Keynesian approach of France; Brunnermeier, James, and Landau 2016). If the decisions must be made unanimously, then it is inevitable that whoever disagrees or is in a minority will use their veto powers to slow down the decision-making process. How is it possible to neutralize veto powers in decision-making processes that require the unanimous consensus of the participants?

At the same time, that crisis amplified in Europe because the intergovernmental constitution could not satisfactorily also respond to the dilemma of respecting the agreements. If financial or fiscal or budgetary policy is based on voluntary coordination among member states, then it is possible that one member state decides not to apply a decision that has been made voluntarily, if that application is no longer convenient for the fortunes of the sitting government. If member states are entrusted with implementing the policy of convergence with the criteria of the Stability and Growth Pact, then it is difficult to check for cheating in regard to the commitments entered into by signing that pact. The failure to respect the commitments did not concern only Greece. Just consider that the commitments of the Stability and Growth Pact had already been abandoned, in 2003, by Germany and France and this had not entailed any penalty for them (Heipertz and Verdun 2010). So why be surprised that a small state does not respect the commitments that not even the biggest states had fulfilled, even if in the case of Greece the failure to meet the commitments took the form of manipulating macroeconomic data, while in the case of the other two countries it was an explicit request to be exonerated from established parameters owing to exceptional circumstances that they had to face (such as, in the case of Germany, national reunification and its costs)?

Nonfulfillment of commitments is a problem that can spiral out of control in a highly interdependent system such as the Eurozone. With the common currency, every choice or non-choice by a state of the Eurozone has an impact on the other members of the Eurozone, creating financial effects that are hard to neutralize (Dyson 2008). Again, the intergovernmental constitution was unable to provide the institutional or policy instruments to contain these effects – so much so, that only the European Central Bank, i.e., a supranational institution, could act effectively in neutralizing financial speculation around the euro (Bastasin 2015; Henning 2016).

Finally, the intergovernmental decision-making process, in a condition of crisis, exacerbated its legitimacy's deficit, leading to the emergence of a hierarchy within the European Council, with the formation of a Franco-German *directoire* for the financial policy of the Eurozone, then becoming solely German as of 2012. After all, if the decisions are made solely by the heads of government within the European Council or by finance ministers within the ECOFIN Council some countries have greater weight than others. Thus, the economic force and political cohesion of Germany ended up imposing the needs of this country on those of the others. Moreover, Germany had, right from the start of the euro crisis, a precise (and convenient) interpretation of the latter's causes, from which followed that the crisis could be resolved only with recessionary policies aimed at reducing public debt. These policies, moreover, were hinged on inflexible legal regulations. This interpretation reflected a genuine economic (and monetary) ideology, the ideology of the country's financial establishment and particularly of its central bank, probably still suffering because of the downsizing of its role with the creation of the European Central Bank (Issing 2008; James 2012).

The fact is that, in any case, within an intergovernmental body, it is inevitable (particularly in a crisis situation, the solution of which has implications in terms of distribution) that hierarchical logic become institutionalized, that the stronger may impose themselves on the weaker. Moreover, France, with its enormous public sector and with an economy blocked by various state and corporative limitations, was no longer able to counterbalance the weight of Germany. Indeed, the fear of losing the latter's support drove France to accept much of Germany's economic ideology. Why be surprised that this *directoire* was then a source of resentment for the citizens of the debtor countries, who found themselves suffering the consequences of policies decided by heads of government for whom they had not voted? The outcome of this process consisted of a Eurozone increasingly centralized and invasive regarding the debtor member states, although such centralization was barely effective and bereft of the basic prerequisites of democracy to legitimize its decisions. Hence there developed the widespread dissatisfaction among the citizens of southern European countries toward the policies being pursued and the methods adopted to decide them. Anti-Europeanism spread like wildfire in all the member states of the Eurozone, in the states of the debtor south (owing to the excessive costs incurred to square their public accounts and recover competitiveness) and in the states of the creditor north (owing to the help sought to support or to consider it necessary to support the debtor countries). Thus, a real paradox has been created: On the institutional side, the Eurozone has further integrated, even if not supranationalized (Fabbrini and Puetter 2016), while on the social side, its member states have further divided. This paradox is the result of the confused model adopted for managing the Eurozone. Indeed, interdependence does not necessarily imply centralization and hierarchy (Eriksen 2017).

Response to Intergovernmental Dilemmas

To respond to these dilemmas, within the intergovernmental constitution, an unprecedented series of key institutional and political decisions has been made since 2010 to manage the financial crisis and to prevent its recurring in the future. The result has been the formation of an intergovernmental union within the EU, increasingly integrated but also increasingly centralized. At least four rounds of decisions must be noted (Fabbrini 2015a; Matthijs and Blyth 2015; Wallace 2016).

The first round took place between 2010 and the first half of 2011. At the ECOFIN Council of May 2010, a regulation was adopted to set up the European Financial Stability Mechanism (EFSM) as a new financial instrument organized within the EU legal order. Very soon, however, it was followed by the European Financial Stability Facility (EFSF), located outside the legal framework of the EU, as an intergovernmental financial instrument to help Ireland and Portugal handle their sovereign debt crises. In September of the same year, the ECOFIN Council approved the European Semester to strengthen the convergence and supervision of the budget policies of the member states of the EU and to make them consistent with the parameters established by the Stability and Growth Pact. The European Semester came into force in January 2011. If the EFSF was a crisis management instrument, the European Semester is an instrument for crisis prevention. Between the European Council of March 24–25 and the European Council of June 23–24 of the same year, crucial legislative measures were also approved, starting with the so-called Six Pack: measures aimed at further centralizing the coordination of budget policies in keeping with the European Semester and the Stability and Growth Pact. The measures of this legislative package came into force in December 2011. In this period, the Euro Plus Pact was also approved, a sort of intergovernmental agreement between the states of the Eurozone and some countries outside of it, with the aim of further deepening the coordination of national economic policies. The signatories of the Euro Plus Pact made a commitment, through concrete choices, to realize a series of structural reforms aimed at improving the competitiveness of their economies and strengthening their fiscal capacity.

The second round of decisions took place between the second half of 2011 and 2012. In July 2011, a first version of an intergovernmental treaty called the European Stability Mechanism (ESM) was signed, a treaty that was then renegotiated and redefined from July of that year to September of the following year, with the task of taking the place of the EFSF, thus becoming a permanent financial instrument to support the countries of the Eurozone that were the target of financial speculation on their sovereign debt. On December 16, 2010, the European Council agreed on an amendment to the TFEU Art. 136. The amendment authorized the member states of the Eurozone to set up a specific intergovernmental treaty, subsequently signed by the then twenty-seven member states of the EU. With this treaty, an international organization was set up based in Luxembourg that provides financial assistance to the states of the Eurozone that are in financial difficulty. Having had to wait for the decision of the German Constitutional Court on the congruence of the ESM with the German constitution, a (positive) decision was finally reached on September 12, 2012, and the ESM finally came into force in January 2013. The ESM acts as a permanent financial firewall with a maximum capacity of €500 billion. The ESM replaces the two previous and temporary financing programs: the (supranational) European Financial Stability Facility (EFSF) and the (intergovernmental) European Financial

Stabilization Mechanism (EFSM). All the new requests for aid from states of the Eurozone connected to financial stability needs will therefore be subject to the ESM, while the EFSF and the EFSM have continued to manage the monitoring of the previous loans given to Ireland, Portugal, and Greece (until their conclusion during 2014). The ESM is governed by a board of directors that makes decisions on a qualified majority basis (at least 80 percent of the total from the contribution of each state that signed the treaty). Because Germany can claim more than 27 percent of the total amount, it will therefore be impossible for the board to make decisions contrary to that country's opinion. The ESM too has been placed outside the legal system of the Lisbon Treaty.

Other crucial decisions were made in 2011, particularly at the European Council of December 8–9 of that year. In that council, the German and French governments proposed to amend the Lisbon Treaty for integrating the fiscal policies of the member states, with the introduction of automatic sanctions against member states that cannot comply with the even stricter criteria of the reformed Stability and Growth Pact: i.e., 0.5 percent public deficit/GDP ratio and 60 percent public debt/GDP ratio. For those member states with public debt to GDP of over 60 percent, it was decided that every year the difference between the public debt/GDP ratio and the 60 percent limit would be reduced by one-twentieth. Finally, it was proposed that the member states introduce, at a constitutional level or with a law of equivalent importance, the balanced budget rule. However, the United Kingdom's opposition to fiscal integration (justified by the defense of the City's financial interests) blocked the proposal to amend the Lisbon Treaty (which would have required unanimity). Given the British position, it was therefore decided to formalize those proposals in a new intergovernmental treaty, again outside the Lisbon Treaty, which was given the name of Treaty on the Stability, Coordination and Governance in the Economic and Monetary Union, better known as the Fiscal Compact. The latter is a treaty signed by twenty-five of the then twenty-seven member states of the EU on March 2, 2012, excluding the United Kingdom and the Czech Republic. The Fiscal Compact formalizes the request to its signatories to introduce constitutional or equivalent laws to guarantee that public budgets are at breakeven or in surplus. These laws must be constitutional in nature to activate self-correcting mechanisms (within the signatory states) so as to prevent breach of the agreement. The Fiscal Compact defines a balanced budget as one with a public deficit of less than 3 percent of GDP and a structural deficit of less than 0.5 percent or 1 percent of GDP, depending on the ratio of public debt to GDP of the signatory country. If the structural deficit exceeds the limit, then the country in question must introduce immediate corrections on the basis of the time frames, objectives, and actions established by the European Commission. The Fiscal Compact puts every signatory state under the jurisdiction of the European Court of Justice, which may impose on states that do not respect the agreement a financial penalty of up to 0.1 percent of their GDP.

The third round of decisions took place between 2013 and 2014. The European Council of June 28–29 and the European Council of December 13–14, 2012, had already provided the basis for a change, albeit relative, in strategy. If the agenda of the European Council of June focused on fiscal rigor, nonetheless it opened the way to recognizing the importance of growth, so much so that the agenda of the European Council in December finally addressed the problem of economic growth and not just of fiscal consolidation. On the basis of a report of the Four Presidents (of the European Council, with a coordinating role, the Commission, the European Central Bank, and the Eurogroup), "Towards a Genuine Economic and Monetary Union" (Van Rompuy 2012), the European Council on December 13–14, 2012, started the formation of a banking union in order to separate banks from sovereign debts (Carmassi, Di Noia, and Micossi 2012). This banking union is based on three pillars: a Single Supervisory Mechanism, a Single Resolution Mechanism, and a common guarantee deposit system (the European Deposit Insurance Scheme, EDIS). The member states of the Eurozone automatically take part in the banking union, while other states can join only if they make a request to do so. The Bank Recovery and Resolution Directive, which was approved in May 2014 by the Council of Ministers and by the European Parliament, then defined the terms for maintaining financial stability and resolving banking crises. During 2013, the first pillar was finalized and approved, the Single Supervisory Mechanism of the main systemic banks of the Eurozone, located within the European Central Bank and coming into operation as of November 2014, while the second pillar became operative as of January 2016. In addition, in 2014, a new intergovernmental treaty was negotiated to create a Single Resolution Fund for banking crises, a fund that will only reach its full financial capacity in 2023 (Veron 2015). In May 2013, a further package of measures came into force (the Two Pack), destined to increase control over national budget policies by the Commission within the indications established by the European Council.

Finally, the fourth round of decisions took place after 2014. In an increasingly divisive economic context between the member states of the Eurozone, the discussion on the reform of the Stability and Growth Pact and on the conclusion of the third pillar of the banking union became inflamed as never before. Several countries (mainly in the south) seriously questioned the ordo-liberal orthodoxy, also thanks to the pressure from the US presidency of Barack Obama. At the time, the logic of the *Spitzenkandidat* had helped Commission president Juncker claim a political, and not merely a technical, role in the interpretation of the Stability and Growth Pact. The requests, by various member states, to use the flexibility clauses of that pact for exceptional reasons led to a more flexible and pragmatic interpretation of the so-called Maastricht parameters. In reality, the restrictions of the Fiscal Compact were quietly ignored, given an economic situation that continued to stagnate. The policy of quantitative easing pursued by the European Central Bank, which aimed to put an increasing quantity of money into the market to push up the inflation rate, did manage to support the necessary economic recovery in the southern countries of the Eurozone, with the northern countries criticizing it. Indeed, crucial German domestic institutions have continued to oppose the European Central Bank's decision to save the euro by doing "whatever it takes." The German Constitutional Court (*Bundesverfassungsgericht*) arrived to submit a request to the European Court of Justice concerning the legality of the Outright Monetary Transaction (OMT), a program designed by the European Central Bank at the height of the euro crisis, accompanying the request with the specification that it should remain free either to accept or to refuse the decision of the European Court of Justice. The OMT is a program under which the European Central Bank makes purchases in secondary sovereign bond markets, under certain conditions, of bonds issued by Eurozone member states (Fabbrini F. 2015). The European Court of Justice, in its June 16, 2015, judgment in *Gauweiler*, backed the legitimacy of the program decided by the European Central Bank, against the opinion of the German Constitutional Court (which then accepted the decision).

The contrast of interests between the member states of the south and the north of the Eurozone also exploded in relation to the construction of the third and final pillar of the banking union. Despite the invitation to speed up that construction (via a new report by the now Five Presidents, as the group also included the president of the European Parliament, this time coordinated by the president of the Commission and published in June 2015; Juncker et al. 2015), the German government continued to put up strong resistance to the idea of sharing the risks at the level of the banking union before reductions had taken place at the level of the individual national banking systems. In November 2015, the Commission presented a legislative proposal to set up a common deposit guarantee system, similar to the models that already existed at national level, but this proposal has remained in paper form only. Indeed, the Commission has continued to pressure for "completing" the Eurozone's financial infrastructure (Epstein and Rhodes 2016), but those proposals haven't moved on, especially once the economic recovery of the Eurozone has subtracted urgency from the European Council's agenda. As Jones (2015: 45) argued, "The failure to construct common institutions to safeguard European financial markets was a mistake."

I have gone back over this long and almost interminable sequence of decisions (and non-decisions) to show their double feature: the regulatory centralization of policy making in the Eurozone and the growing divisions between the latter's member states (on this, see Caporaso and Rhodes 2016). We have seen the construction of a centralized system of administrative regulation of financial and budgetary policies of the individual member states of the Eurozone, a system based on respecting formal criteria independent from empirical reality (Matthijs 2016). With the inclusion of the Stability and Growth Pact in the treaties, economic policy has been judicialized. The judicialization of economic policy could not accommodate the different political economies of the Eurozone's member states. Lacking the necessary degree of political discretion in economic policy choices, and in the absence of reciprocal trust between the member states, the economic governance's model of the Eurozone has come to be based on automatic mechanisms of fiscal regulation and legal rules to supervise national policies, i.e., administrative centralization without political democratization. National democracies have been laid bare, and no supranational democracy has been created. Political discretion has been abolished as a concept to be replaced with technical procedures established in advance.

Economic policy has become independent from the economic cycle, contrary to what it should be. The fiscal sovereignty of each member state has been formally preserved but, for neutralizing the possibility of moral hazard, a centralized system of fiscal regulation, highly intrusive in national fiscal sovereignty, has been set up. This is the worst of two worlds. Of course, such centralized integration has not occurred within the supranational constitution of the single market. An intergovernmental order has been formed that has ended up conflicting with the supranational order.

Intergovernmental Governance of the Migration Crisis

Similar characteristics have been seen in the governance of migration policy. In Maastricht, this policy was assigned to the third pillar (that of Justice and Home Affairs, or JHA) marked by the same intergovernmental logic of the second pillar (that of the Common Foreign and Security Policy, or CFSP). The objective of the third pillar was that of facilitating coordination between the national governments on cross-border issues, as well as between their national judicial policies. The cross-border issues include the protection of fundamental rights, the free movement of citizens, civil protection and combating people trafficking, the issues linked to immigration and to requests for political asylum, the inquiries into transnational organized crime and cooperation between police and national intelligence branches, and security policies understood as opposing terrorism and cybercrime. Originally, these policies were decided in accordance with a strictly intergovernmental approach, which was institutionalized in the council coordinating home affairs and justice ministers. Nonetheless, the growing complexity of those policies and the need to acquire higher efficiency levels in combating terrorism and in intelligence investigations have gradually led to an increasingly influential role for the Commission. That role has grown so much that there has been talk of a gradual supranationalization of the third pillar, a supranationalization then given form by the Lisbon Treaty that brought back many decisions in the field of justice and home affairs to the ordinary legislative procedure (i.e., proposal by the Commission and co-decision by the European Parliament and the Council of Ministers). Nonetheless, with the explosion of the migration crisis in the mid-2010s, the Council of Ministers (and in turn the European Council) took over control of decision-making (not only on migration policy but also on political asylum policy). In order to do this, it used a special procedure by virtue of which the European Parliament may be consulted and the Commission may be requested to present proposals, but neither of them can be involved in the final decision. Moreover, regarding political asylum, the continuing existence of the Dublin Convention, given the mass arrival of political refugees in Europe as an effect of the Syrian crisis between 2014 and 2016, accentuated the impact of those arrivals on some countries, the handling of which national governments did not wish to entrust to the Commission. The effects of that immigration have been dramatic, to the point of putting wind into the sails of anti-Europeanist forces in the national elections held in various European countries.

Let us take a closer look at what the Dublin Convention implies. The Dublin Convention is an international treaty that regulates the rights of political asylum in the European countries that have signed it. The principle that underpins it is as follows: It is the responsibility of the country where the refugee first arrives to handle the formalization of their status. More generally, it is the duty of the country of first arrival to distinguish between immigrants who have the right to be recognized as refugees and immigrants who do not have such a right (and who must therefore be sent back to their country of origin). The burden of handling the problem is entirely on the shoulders of individual national governments, thus marking the exclusively intergovernmental nature of political asylum policy. The Convention was signed on June 15, 1990, in Dublin by twelve countries (Belgium, Denmark, France, Germany, Greece, Ireland, Italy, Luxembourg, the Netherlands, Portugal, Spain, and the United Kingdom) and became effective seven years later, on September 1, 1997. In the same year, Austria, Sweden (as of October 1, 1997), and Finland (as of January 1, 1998) adopted the Dublin Convention. With this first agreement, Europe tried to provide due assistance to political refugees by creating an international regulation for political asylum requests, based on the Geneva Convention of 1951 and on the New York Protocol of 1967. Given the changes in migration flows, in 2003 the EU revised the Dublin Convention, changing some sections and renaming it Dublin Convention 2. With this latter agreement, a databank was created at the European level for inputting the digital fingerprints of those who request political asylum in member states.

The mass arrival in Europe of refugees from crisis areas and failing states in the Middle East then led to a further revision, the so-called Dublin Convention 3, which was signed in June 2013 and came into force on July 19 of that year. This revision was signed by all the states that had already signed the original Dublin Convention, with the sole exception of Denmark. Despite the various revisions, the logic of the Dublin Convention was not, however, changed: Political asylum requests must be processed by the first state where the immigrant arrives. The latter must request political asylum in the state where they arrive, and it is that state which has exclusive competence to respond to the request. In addition, if the political refugee moves to another country, the latter must send them back to the state where they arrived as an immigrant, in other words, where they presented their political asylum request. This has produced important consequences for countries such as Italy and Greece. They not only have had to take responsibility for processing hundreds of thousands of immigrants arriving from Africa, but also have had to take back these immigrants when they moved to other countries of the EU. Moreover, the European databank has enabled the authorities of the individual countries to verify more precisely where the first request was made.

Despite the signatory states to the Dublin Convention having shared a databank on the digital fingerprints of clandestine immigrants who request political asylum, political asylum policy has continued to be an exclusively national responsibility. The state that first accepts the non-EU citizen must take responsibility for establishing whether they have the prerequisites to put forward a political asylum request, then providing accommodation to the applicant. Here, "take responsibility" means that the state in question must use its own financial, administrative, and organizational resources to handle the problem. This has created disparities among political refugees and among states. Such disparities are so unjustifiable as to drive international organizations such as the United Nations High Commissioner for Refugees (UNHCR), the European Council on Refugees and Exiles (a pan-European alliance of ninety NGOs protecting and advancing the rights of refugees, asylum seekers, and displaced persons), as well as the Commissioner for Human Rights of the Council of Europe, to criticize the procedures of the Dublin Convention. As of 2015, a dramatic year owing to the deaths at sea of groups of immigrants who were trying to reach European coasts, many states have decided to suspend application of the Dublin Convention in their territory. This has driven the initiative of the Commission to submit, on September 9, 2015, an action plan for the reallocation of 120,000 refugees (located mainly in Italy and Greece) in the other member states of the EU, a reallocation based on objective variables (such as the country's GDP, the number of inhabitants, and growth rate).

The Commission's proposal was then approved (following the special legislative procedure) by a qualified majority of the Council of Ministers for Justice and Home Affairs, having received the positive opinion of the European Parliament. Moreover, in a joint speech to the European Parliament on October 7, 2015, the German chancellor Angela Merkel and the French president François Hollande stressed the need to create a Dublin Convention 4 to formalize a common and no longer national approach to the handling of political asylum. In a meeting of the European Council held in Valletta the following November, the reallocation strategy was, however, contested by a few heads of government, particularly of the countries of eastern Europe. Above all, they contested the Commission's project of creating a permanent mechanism of solidarity between the member states, by virtue of which the reallocation would take place automatically in the future. This project would have to be approved through the ordinary legislative procedure, based on a qualified majority of the Council of Ministers and an absolute majority of the European Parliament. Two eastern countries (Hungary and Slovakia) appealed the European Court of Justice in late 2015 against the Council of Ministers' decision to relocate refugees from Italy and Greece. Although the European Court of Justice, in its decision of September 2017, dismissed the action of the two countries, nevertheless, the relocation's mechanism has continued to be opposed by the eastern member states, notwithstanding the Commission's decision in June 2017 to open an infringement procedure against the Czech Republic, Hungary, and Poland for noncompliance with their obligation under the relocation's mechanism. In its meeting of December 2017, the European Council, under the pressure of its president (the Pole Donald Tusk), was asked to reconsider the entire EU refugee policy.

Mass economic and political immigration overturned the consensus that had led not only to the Dublin Convention but also to the Schengen agreements under which an area of free circulation of people was created corresponding to the states that signed those agreements (we should recall that those agreements, signed by some countries

in June 1985 as an international treaty, then became primary law of the
EU with the Treaty of Amsterdam of 1999). Because Schengen abolished internal borders without protecting external borders,
in December 2015, the European Council finally approved, with the
consent of the European Parliament, the Commission's proposal to
transform Frontex (an agency tasked with functions of supporting
national border control) into the more organized and staffed
European Border and Coast Guard (officially launching it
on October 6, 2016, at the Bulgarian external border with Turkey).
However, the new agency also has the assignment of supporting member states facing massive migration influx and not to pursue its own
independent initiative. Indeed, given unprecedented immigration as of
2015, fully six member states of the EU (starting with Germany)
decided to suspend, albeit temporarily, free circulation in their territory, reintroducing forms of border control. Both the Dublin and
Schengen agreements have shown how intergovernmental consensus
can be called into question by crises that have distributive effects on the
various member states, and above all with regard to issues (such as
immigration) that have a significant impact on the electoral fortunes of
sitting governments. The result is that migration policy and political
asylum policy have ended up creating further divisions within the EU,
between the member states of first arrival and the others, between the
member states willing to take responsibility for reallocation of the
refugees and the member states opposed to doing so, between rich
and less rich member states. Territorial sovereignty as well as fiscal
sovereignty have remained under the formal control of member states.

Intergovernmental Logic and Domestic Political Deconstruction

Bound by intergovernmental logic, the EU (and the Eurozone particularly) has had to introduce a striking number of decisions and institutions that have sent the integration process into a tailspin. This tailspin,
even if it has seen greater integration of the Eurozone, has done so
without guaranteeing either the effectiveness or the legitimacy of the
decisions made and of the institutions created. Because the intergovernmental logic cannot provide a satisfactory response to basic dilemmas
of interstate cooperation, the result has been a multiplication of intergovernmental treaties (such as the European Stability Mechanism, the

Fiscal Compact, and the Single Resolution Fund for banking crises) aimed at legalizing the terms of that cooperation. The objectives that have been sought with these treaties could have been achieved with the instruments already envisaged by the Lisbon Treaty (such as enhanced cooperation) or with an extension of the supranational constitution to the sectors of economic and financial policy (as happened with the approval of the Six Pack and of the Two Pack with which the coordination system of the Stability and Growth Pact was strengthened). However, the intergovernmental logic has not allowed this possibility. Because unanimity is necessary to amend the Lisbon Treaty, the veto of one or two member states (the United Kingdom and the Czech Republic) was sufficient to block the reform of fiscal policy, thus obliging the other member states to go toward a new intergovernmental treaty, the Fiscal Compact. Having moved outside the legal order of the EU, the governments of the biggest countries had to use anti-intergovernmental remedies against the defects of the intergovernmental agreement. To prevent the possibility that one member state might vote against approval of the Fiscal Compact (in a referendum or in parliament), thus stopping it from coming into force, it was decided that it could come into force on January 1, 2013 (as happened) if approved by only twelve (of the then seventeen states of the Eurozone). In addition, to avoid the danger that was seen with the Lisbon Treaty, which was blocked by a small country (Ireland) for over a year, it was decided that any member state that voted against the Fiscal Compact would not be able to benefit from the financial cover guaranteed by the European Stability Mechanism in the case of speculation on its sovereign debt.

Thus, the intergovernmental logic was established and then cut back immediately. For example, with the decision to introduce, in the constitutions of the contracting states, the balanced budget amendment, the role of national constitutional courts was strengthened. At the same time, with the Fiscal Compact, automatic mechanisms were introduced to act on member states that do not respect the established parameters, mechanisms that can be activated by the Commission or by any other member state that has adhered to the treaty. In both cases, an appeal can be made to the European Court of Justice, which can impose fines on defaulting states. Thus, in order to avoid a repetition of the situation in 2003 (when Germany and France were exonerated from the costs of defaulting on the Stability and Growth Pact with a decision of the

ECOFIN Council) and also to avoid experiences such as the subsequent case of Greece (which defaulted on the Stability and Growth Pact manipulating national data on public deficit and debt), it was decided to reduce the discretional power of the intergovernmental bodies themselves (European Council and Council of Ministers) to strengthen the technical capacity of the Commission, and to transform the European Court of Justice into a kind of administrative court that imposes financial sanctions on defaulting states. Thus, a decision by the Commission to open an infraction procedure against a defaulting state in regard to the commitments required by the Stability and Growth Pact is now automatically activated, unless it is halted by a reverse qualified majority of the ECOFIN Council. Because national governments do not trust each other, a system has been constructed that is focused on policy rules transformed into a legal order. But, of course, a system of legal rules and automatic administrative procedures cannot take into consideration the economic reality of the moment or the different economic realities of the member states.

This regulatory centralization could not fail to raise political problems at the domestic level. Intergovernmental centralization has ended up undermining national politics focused on the competition between right and left, thus opening space for the rise of populist movements and nationalist forces across the continent. Almost everywhere in Europe the traditional parties are struggling. The decline of these parties (Christian Democrats, Social Democrats, Liberal Democrats) has gone on in parallel with the rise of anti-EU movements, i.e., of movements with a strong anti-integration stance. It has followed that the competition between right and left has proved increasingly unable to reabsorb at the domestic level the dissatisfaction and unrest of one or another group of electors. In the long post–Second World War period, that competition had stabilized the drive for social change that cyclically flowered in the electorate, drawing it toward one or another party of right or left. The competition between the latter had absolved a quasi-constitutional function, bringing back within democratic politics the reaction to social change, including the most radical, which emerged from society. The competition between the right and left had thus helped create the political infrastructure for the post-war economic development of European countries, thus guaranteeing support for the integration process (Mair 2013).

With the consolidation of intergovernmental governance, that political competition has not worked as well as previously. Following the 2008 financial crisis and the formation of a consensus within the intergovernmental institutions, the distinction between right and left has become blurred in almost all national political systems. The deeper the crisis has become, the more left and right have had to draw closer around the established consensus. A real policy convergence has occurred between political forces that were traditionally, and proudly, adversarial. This convergence has sometimes been institutionalized in grand coalition governments, wherein the electoral system and the form of government made what occurred in Germany possible (which had a grand coalition in the period 2005–2009, then again in the period 2013–2017, and finally after 2018) and in other countries (as in the Netherlands) with a proportional electoral system and a parliamentary form of government. But things did not go any differently in a country such as France, with its majority electoral system and semi-presidential form of government, which formally precludes the formation of coalition governments involving the right and left. Indeed, in that country, with the success of Emmanuel Macron in the May 2017 presidential elections and of his new-formed party (*Republic en marche*) in the June 2017 parliamentary elections, an informal coalition government, aggregating politicians from both moderate left and right, was set up by the president. The pressure to remain within the judicialized parameters established at the Eurozone level has reduced the room to differentiate oneself at the national level.

If the competition between left and right has increasingly lost political significance, then the contradictions and inequalities caused by integration have ended up finding new channels to connect with politics. It is the populist movements that have put themselves forward to respond to those effects, directing public opinion not only toward rejection of traditional parties (right and left) but above all toward rejecting the EU of which these parties are (and were) the political infrastructure. A new division has thus been created between the traditional establishment (including the moderate right and moderate left) and the new political actors. The latter have been successful when they have managed to obscure the distinction between the rejection of an integrated Europe as such and the criticism of its policies. Particularly in the Eurozone's countries, there has been a radical change in the structure of political competition. Driven by economic necessities, choices have been made at the Eurozone level without evaluating their political consequences at the member state level. A system has been created to manage the Eurozone in which the decisions on the most important economic policies have been protected from any supranational electoral process. In Brussels, those decisions are made by intergovernmental bodies (such as the European Council or the Council of Ministers) consisting of a collection of national leaders driven to act on the basis of agreements that require the convergence of their originally distinctive positions. If they abandon those agreements, they expose their country to the reaction of the markets and to isolation compared with the other European partners. If they remain on the perimeter of those agreements, they fuel the anti-Europeanist reaction of the populist parties in their own country.

If intergovernmental integration cannot function in terms of the effectiveness of the decisions made, even less so can it satisfy the need to guarantee their legitimacy. The new treaties, by the very fact of their intergovernmental nature, have not resolved, nor could they have resolved, the problems of legitimizing the decisions made by and in the intergovernmental bodies (of the European Council and the Council of Ministers). Indeed, those decisions have been made and continue to be made excluding the European Parliament, the institution that represents the electors who must bear the weight of the practical effects of those decisions. As Schmidt (2015: 111) observed, the European Parliament "has largely been excluded from most decisions on the euro by EU treaties, as well as in cases where international institutions have been involved." Certainly, there has been no lack of statements by government leaders who argued that they were able to make those decisions because they were legitimated by their national electorates. Such statements are, nonetheless, hard to justify from the viewpoint of democratic legitimacy. National electorates have chosen their national governments to make national decisions. But when these governments act in Brussels, they make decisions that have implications for the electorates of other countries, and not only for their own national electorate. Legitimacy does not transfer from the national level to the European level. The decisions made at the European level must be legitimated by institutions representing European electorates (such as, specifically, the European Parliament), while decisions made at the national level must be legitimated by institutions representing the national electorates (such as, specifically, national parliaments).

Thus, with the transfer of decision-making to Brussels, there has been a weakening of the capacity of national parliaments to control their respective national governments, without this weakening being compensated by a strengthening of the capacity of the European Parliament to control the collectivity of national governments that operate within the intergovernmental bodies of the EU. Because the decisions made by and within the intergovernmental institutions imply the consent of national leaders constituting them, it will be unlikely that the political majority within the various national parliaments would contest choices also made by their national leaders. Logically, the intergovernmental approach would require interparliamentarism for being checked. But, empirically, this possibility is not in the order of things. Indeed, if the national governments of the largest and strongest member states have been more influential in intergovernmental decisions, the same might happen for the national parliaments of the largest and strongest member states. The intergovernmental logic has created hierarchies not only between national governments but also between national parliaments. Therefore, how can we consider as legitimate a decision made under the pressure of one influential member state, but the effects of which also affect the citizens of the other member states?

It would be wrong, as well as ungenerous, to argue that the EU has not tried to react to the challenges of the financial markets. Nonetheless, its responses have come within an intergovernmental model whose logic has not only been confirmed but also strengthened. As Jones, Kelemen, and Meunier (2016: 1012) argued, EU leaders certainly "took steps toward deeper integration to preserve the euro, [but they] have acted much as they did at the inception of the common currency: repeatedly putting in place incomplete, unsustainable solutions and rejecting more comprehensive, reform proposals." Thus, the euro crisis has produced more integration in the Eurozone, but the latter has not assumed supranational characteristics, as happened in the past (when crises occurred in the single market). There has been integration without democratization. Integration has not been accompanied by the strengthening of the supranational institutions (and of the European Parliament in particular). The intergovernmental treaties and legislative measures have recognized the decision-making primacy of national governments, so much so that, for example, the objectives that it was hoped to achieve with these treaties could have been achieved with the instruments already envisaged by the Lisbon

Treaty, such as enhanced cooperation. The latter, however, would have required the involvement of the Commission and of the European Parliament, involvement that was not desired by many national governments. Thus, if it is true that some measures, aimed at strengthening surveillance over national budgets, were approved through the ordinary legislative procedure (such as the Six Pack in 2011 and the Two Pack in 2013) (Dehousse 2016; Laffan 2014), nonetheless these decisions were made in the shadow of the European Council (Bressanelli and Chelotti 2016), and in any case their legislative contents did not call into question the intergovernmental logic based on the centrality of the European Council. Of course, it cannot be denied that the new treaties, particularly the Fiscal Compact, have introduced important procedural innovations. For example, for the Fiscal Compact to come into force, unanimity was no longer necessary (and it is the first time this has happened in the history of European treaties) or the disciplinary skills of supranational institutions were enhanced (such as the Commission and the European Court of Justice) for ensuring the fulfillment of the agreements made by the contracting states (even if, again, the decision of the Commission can be neutralized by a reversed majority of the ECOFIN Council). Nonetheless, those innovations could not resolve the internal and external legitimacy limits of intergovernmental decisions – external, because the decisions are made excluding control by the European Parliament, and internal, because the decisions are exposed to the pressure of the biggest and strongest states (when crucial policies – for them – are at stake). This is why the economic governance of the Eurozone has continued to be more controversial than ever.

Conclusion

When in Maastricht, between 1991 and 1992, national governments were forced to Europeanize strategic policies, they decided to do so provided that supranational institutions (such as the European Parliament, the Commission, and the European Court of Justice itself) were excluded from the decision-making process. Intergovernmental pillars were thus devised for deciding those policies. Many thought (then) that the intergovernmental approach for those policies would, sooner or later, pass to a supranational logic. They were wrong. National governments showed themselves to be far from willing to transfer the handling of issues crucial for their electoral destiny (such as fiscal, refugee, or security policy) to EU institutions that are not controlled by them, such as the Commission or the European Parliament. Indeed, with the multiple crises of the 2010s, the control of national governments over strategic policies has become even stronger – thus producing a paradoxical result. In crisis conditions, in fact, national governments cannot make effective decisions, because their interests conflict and the resources are limited, hence the public expectation on the rise of powerful national leaders to make up for intergovernmental weaknesses. But, how can anyone reasonably think that a leader, elected to pursue the interests of their own country, becomes the supranational champion of Europe's interests? The result has been that strategic policies, which are at the center of national conflicts, have seen recurrent paralysis at the European level. The more this paralysis became institutionalized, the more citizens turned to national solutions, ending up also calling into question what worked well (such as the single market, in fact). Without a distinct (from the national level) governmental capacity, the EU cannot neutralize the centrifugal forces and periodic stalemates coming from national governmental rivalries.

The transformations induced in the functioning of the EU by the multiple crises of the 2010s and by Brexit raise new institutional problems and unexpected challenges in interpretation. The intergovernmental EU that emerged from those crises has little to do with the supranational EU that organizes the functioning of the single market. In the policies to address the crises of the 2010s, national governments have occupied the center of the decision-making process, even if they have not been able to exclude the Commission from the latter. We have seen the institutionalization of a decision-making system that is highly centralized and that has accentuated the divisions between the member states, each of them worried about defending or imposing their own electoral interests (presented as national interests). Have we gone back to the experience of the Vienna Congress of 1815, at which independent states sought to negotiate a new European equilibrium, a stable and reciprocally advantageous equilibrium (Kissinger 1956)? Of course not, because the intergovernmental EU is much more than a diplomatic arena.

Nonetheless, there is no doubt that the intergovernmental governance of the multiple crises has brought to the fore divisions between member states that are incompatible with the inspiration at the basis of the integration process, that is, according to the declaration delivered by the French foreign affairs minister Robert Schuman on May 9, 1950, to lay the "foundation of a European federation indispensable to the preservation of peace." Nor has that management been compatible with what German chancellor Angela Merkel said sixty years later, on November 2, 2010, at the ceremony to inaugurate the sixty-first academic year of the College of Europe in Bruges. On that occasion, Merkel said, "The Lisbon Treaty has placed the institutional structure [of the EU] on a new foundation," to the point of rendering outdated the traditional distinctions between "Community and intergovernmental methods." Indeed, she added, the EU is already functioning according to a "new Union method," which consists of "coordinated action in a spirit of solidarity." Rather than solidarity, hierarchies between member states have been visible in those crises. Such hierarchies are in contradiction to the aim of continental integration launched in Paris in 1952 and in Rome in 1957, i.e., the creation of a union among equals as celebrated by TEU Art. 4(2): "The Union shall respect the equality of Member States before the Treaties."

The intergovernmental governance of the multiple crises has deepened the opposition to the EU and its policies, triggering the resurgence of nationalist and populist movements all over Europe, with different implications in the east and the west. There is a correlation, rather than a causation, between the intergovernmental logic adopted by the EU in crucial policies and the populist and nationalist (or sovereignist) reaction to them that deserves to be investigated. It has to be investigated whether the growth of sovereignist forces has been the result of contingent factors or rather the expression of deeper currents of national public opinion (activated by the crises and their governance). Indeed, the multiple crises have shown the existence of deep political faults between member states regarding the finality of the integration process. Although the sovereignist forces do not seem to follow the British path (because of its high economic and political costs), they, however, claim the return to an economic community, a continental market organization considered compatible with the preservation of national sovereignty. At the same time, particularly within the Eurozone member states, Macron's program to build "a sovereign, united and democratic Europe" has advanced an alternative agenda, relaunching the perspective of a political union (epitomized by the clause of an "ever closer union"). Although the distinction between the perspectives of an economic or political union does not reflect the intricacies of the integration's process, nevertheless it can help to delineate the long-term divergence between member states with regard to the aims of the integration process. The next chapter investigates these issues.

the perspectives of an economic or political union does not reflect proportion..... reflect proportion..... define the long-term divergence between ..... states with regard to the logic of the integration process..... approaches to these issues.

3 | Sovereignist Challenges and the Political Union

Introduction

The multiple crises of the 2010s (and the limits shown by their intergovernmental governance) have brought to the surface an unprecedented nationalist sentiment in many EU member states. Nationalist parties and movements have become influential political actors in the western member states, while they have reached the control of governmental power in the large majority of eastern member states. Exploiting the inability of the EU to guarantee security to its citizens, control of its external borders, and the economic growth of several (Eurozone) member states, nationalism has emerged as a competitive option for re-ordering domestic and EU politics. Indeed, with Brexit, nationalism has arrived to challenge the (so far) dominant narrative of European integration – namely, that the latter will benefit all the participating member states. The resurgence of nationalism has inevitably shaken the orthodox Europeanism shared by domestic and European mainstream elites. This orthodoxy consists of the idea that European integration will inevitably move forward, muddling through crises and their solutions. As Robert Schuman declared on May 9, 1950, "Europe will not be made all at once, or according to a single plan. It will be built through concrete achievements which first create a de facto solidarity." However, the strength of nationalist movements, and their holy alliance with populism, has shown that the supporters of European integration can no longer run away from the necessity of devising a plan for contrasting the new redoubtable adversary. I call *sovereignism* the synthesis of the holy alliance between nationalism and populism and *Europeanism* the alternative position of promoting the project of an "ever closer union."

The cleavage between sovereignism and Europeanism reflects the different perspectives on European integration pursued by different states or regional coalitions of states, differences that have accompanied the process of integration thus made irreconcilable by the multiple crises of the 2010s. These perspectives reflect different national visions of sovereignty and democracy – specifically, how those visions relate to the integration process (Lacroix and Nicolaidis 2010). Although each single national perspective or polity idea (Jachtenfuchs 1995) has its domestic opposition, nevertheless, it reflects attitudes and values shared by public opinions and relevant domestic groups of the concerned country, because of the specific historical experience, geographical location, and national culture of the latter. These differing visions can be regrouped around two fundamental interpretations of the integration process (one economic and the other political), interpretations constructed by domestic elites within a national structured script. Certainly, each fundamental interpretation (economic or political) has been translated differently by one or another country advancing it. Those interpretations may have different tones in different historical circumstances, but they reflect consolidated predispositions that constrain domestic elites' narrative on the integration process. If the economic vision drove toward disintegration in the United Kingdom (with Brexit), this is not necessarily the outcome in other countries sharing that vision. The supporters of economic vision are certainly defenders of national sovereignty, but they assume (or are obliged to assume by reality) that the latter should be compatible with the functioning of an economic community (understood as a regional economic organization). They are against the political finality of an "ever closer union," but not against the process of economic integration per se. They are anti-Europeanists because Europeanism coincides with that political finality, but they are not against economic integration in Europe. They are sovereignists, although the interpretation of sovereignism differs among them, with Brexit representing the radical version of it. The political view of the integration project, too, has been interpreted differently by its various supporters. They all are Europeanists because they share the aim of creating an "ever closer union"; however, some member states have interpreted it as the project of building a parliamentary union, while other member states have come to interpret it as the project of building an executive-based intergovernmental union. Notwithstanding these differences, both

Europeanisms share the same statist paradigm, which assumes the formation of the European polity as the further development of the national polity. Indeed, either in the European Parliament or in the European Council, both political visions accept the necessity of centralizing the decision-making process.

This chapter tries to map this debate. It is organized as follows: First, it investigates the distinctive features of nationalism and populism. Second, it discusses their hodgepodge as sovereignism, particularly in the eastern and central EU member states. Third, it analyzes the economic vision of integration that constitutes the structural background of sovereignism. Fourth, it considers the historical and cultural features of the alternative vision of integration, the political view as expressed by the "ever closer union" clause introducing all EU treaties.

The Holy Alliance between Nationalism and Populism

Nationalist and populist movements and parties have emerged as crucial actors in all the national elections held in the 2010s and in the election for the European Parliament. At the end of the 2010s, the situation is the following: Nationalist parties or coalitions are in control of the government of many eastern and central European countries (Poland, Hungary, Slovakia, and the Czech Republic, the so-called Visegrad Group, as well as Romania and Bulgaria) and they are influential in the Baltics (Latvia in particular). Nationalist parties are influential in western European countries as well, although they are not in power as they are in eastern Europe. However, the nationalist *Freiheitliche Partei Österreichs* (FPÖ) gained control of crucial ministries in the Austrian coalition government after the parliamentary election of October 2017. The nationalist *Alternative für Deutschland* (AfD) resulted in a third party in Germany and the first (in the *Land* of Saxony) or second (in the other four eastern German *Länder*) after the *Bundestag*'s elections of September 2017. The main party of the Belgian coalition government is the nationalist-regionalist party of the New Flemish Alliance, or *Nieuw-Vlaamse Alliantie* (N-VA). In the Netherlands, although the nationalist Freedom Party, or *Partij voor de Vrijheid* (PVV), did not enter the government after the election of March 2017, nevertheless the government that was formed after 208 days of negotiation includes the highly nationalist party called the Christian Union. In Denmark, the government survives through the external support of the nationalist Danish People's Party, or *Dansk*

Folkeparti (DF). In Finland, a faction of the nationalist party of the True Finns (the Blue Reform group) was crucial in keeping the government alive after the June 2017 crisis. In Greece, the conservative-nationalist party of Independent Greeks (ANEL) has been the indispensable partner of the government since 2015. In France, the nationalist leader of the *Front National*, Marine Le Pen, got 33.9 percent of the presidential vote in the elections held in May 2017. In Italy, nationalist parties (League) and populist movements (Five Star Movement) received more than half of the national votes in the elections of March 2018, to the point of forming the first sovereignist government in one of the largest EU member states and an EU founding state. In the election for the European Parliament held in March 2014, nationalist parties got roughly a third of the seats. However, in those elections, Nigel Farage's pro-independence party (UKIP) became the leading party in Great Britain. The same happened for Denmark, with the Danish People's Party becoming the first party in the country, with almost 28 percent of the vote. Albeit in more moderate forms, euro-skepticism was also a feature of the main parties in Sweden. In eastern and central European countries, voters oscillated between indifference toward and rejection of the European Parliament. In those elections, the turnout was 13 percent in Slovakia (which is also part of the Eurozone), 19.5 percent in the Czech Republic (which is not part of the Eurozone), and 25 percent in Croatia (which had just joined the EU). In sum, nationalism has become a dominant force in the northern peninsular and eastern European countries and an influential force in the western continental countries. All over, nationalism has allied with populism for increasing its electoral appeal. How do we interpret this successful upheaval?

The rationale of populist appeal has been different in the various areas of Europe. In many countries of the Eurozone, the populist mobilization has been awakened by a strong anti-establishment feeling. In Greece, Spain, and Italy, the populist movements certainly benefited from the rejection of traditional parties considered corrupt and basically identical. However, those populist movements were also fed by dissatisfaction at the handling of the financial crisis, and its asymmetric consequences (which penalized the peripheral countries of the southern Eurozone more than the countries of the center and the north). It was inevitable for those populist movements to direct this dissatisfaction toward the request for a return to national control over the main public policies (or even, in a few cases, to a return to the old national currencies). On the other hand, in the northern countries of the Eurozone, the populist mobilization was fed by factors that were not strictly economic but were generally related to national identity issues. Here it was immigration, the fear of being invaded by uncontrolled migratory flows, especially from Islamic countries in Africa and Asia, that triggered the populist mobilization. In both cases, populism ended up as a sounding board for nationalist feelings that had long been dormant in those national societies, connecting them to frustration over the management of EU migration policy. In western Europe (and the Eurozone particularly), a new nationalist populism has been affirmed in several of those countries. This populism is considered new, because it connected domestic anti-political sentiment to criticism of the technocratic elites accused of governing the integration process for their own interests (or the interests of multinational firms, transnational banks, cosmopolitan managerial and cultural elites). These technocracies are considered to be insensitive both toward citizens who have paid the price of austerity policies and toward citizens worried about preserving their national identities. And this populism is considered nationalist, because it used criticism of Brussels technocracy to justify the return to national sovereignty as a necessary condition to giving people a say again in crucial policies. Thus, this form of populism has restored legitimacy to nationalism in western Europe's public discourse, after its protracted de-legitimization in the long post-Second World War period. It carries the paradox, however, that, if this re-legitimization is successful, nationalism will again relaunch the role of domestic elites against which populism had originally been mobilized. In any case, identity has become (again) a resource for political mobilization (Fukyama 2018).

The idea that the EU is led by cosmopolitan technocracies, which are not sensitive to the concerns of national citizens, is particularly widespread among the elites of countries outside the Eurozone, both the opt-out countries (of the Scandinavian north) and the countries that are supposed to adopt the euro in the future (of eastern and central Europe). Thus, *nationalist populism* motivated by anti-technocratic criticism within the Eurozone (over how the euro crisis has been managed and over the hierarchies among the states which that management has created) intertwined with *populist nationalism* grown in many of the countries outside the Eurozone, nationalism fed by historical reasons even if triggered by specific choices (particularly in immigration policy). Following the migration crisis of the summer of 2015, the request to close national borders ended up giving rise to a contradictory coalition of populist nationalist groups. It was contradictory because it brought together countries such as the United Kingdom (which eventually decided to leave the EU in order to avoid the obligation of allowing unrestricted entry to citizens from other EU countries) and countries such as Poland, Hungary, the Czech Republic, and Slovakia (which are totally opposed to letting non-European immigrants into their countries, but equally totally in favor of their own citizens being able to emigrate to other countries of the EU, the United Kingdom in particular).

Although allied, however, populism and nationalism are distinct political phenomena (and movements), on both a practical and theoretical level. Populism, as a concept and as a political movement, has accompanied, and sometimes challenged, the process of institutionalizing liberal democracies. Historically, populism has had both democratic and anti-democratic elements, albeit not all anti-democratic movements have been populist (Mény and Surel 2000; Mueller 2016). Both (democratic and anti-democratic) populisms are based on the assumption that the *people* have, and must have, primacy over every power set up (and over those who manage such power, the elite). For populists, the people are (or better, *is*) the sole source of political legitimization. As Judis (2016: 15) observed, "The exact referents of the 'people' and the 'elite' don't define populism: what defines it is the conflictual relationship between the two." Populism, both democratic and anti-democratic, has been, and continues to be, necessarily illiberal because it does not justify limitations, whether constitutional or institutional, introduced by liberalism to regulate the exercise of the popular will. Democratic populism too has had clear difficulty in accepting the division of powers, for the very reason that it disperses and disaggregates the otherwise unitary character of the popular will. "Populists are always *antipluralist* [because they] claim that they, and they alone, represent the people" (Mueller 2016: 3, italics in the original). Over time, democratic populism has ended up accepting liberalism, that is, the constitutional division between powers, even if it has, nonetheless, tried to subordinate that division to the popular will. Hence, permanent tension has regularly re-emerged in liberal democracies between their two founding principles, i.e., the sovereignty of the people and the sovereignty of the constitution. This tension is expressed by the social

contrast between the "many" and the "few," between the popular
masses and the restricted elites identified with the functioning of constitutional institutions. It is no surprise that populism, including democratic populism, is profoundly anti-elitist.

It has not been easy to reconcile the people and the constitution
because the boundary between popular sovereignty and constitutional
sovereignty is anything but set in stone. Indeed, historically, it has
shifted continuously, under the pressure of the coalitions that have
been mobilized, in one case, to expand the exercise of popular power
and, in the other case, to limit that exercise through constitutional
counter-powers. With the development of mass politics, the shift has
favored popular more than constitutional sovereignty, to the extent
that post-Second World War constitutions have become instruments to
empower society, not simply instruments to limit the power of society.
With the constitutionalization of economic and social rights, constitutions have been transformed into charters that have increased the
power of the people, rather than instruments to regulate their political
conduct. Although the contrast between the two conceptions of sovereignty has regularly emerged in democratic countries, nevertheless the
established democracies of western Europe have been able to find an
equilibrium around the acceptance (by the main political actors) of the
role of domestic constitutional courts as solvers of last resort. Where
politics has not been able to interiorize elements that regulate its own
popular character, by submitting the tension between rules and people
under the supervisory role of independent constitutional courts, the
result has been the subordination of the courts (and other independent
institutions) to the will of the people as represented by the incumbent
governments.

Nationalism, too, just like populism, has had both democratic and
anti-democratic aspects. This duplicity has historically manifested itself
within each individual European country, but with very significant
differences between countries and regional areas. In the islands and
peninsulas of northern Europe (in the United Kingdom, but also in
Scandinavia), nationalism has historically maintained a democratic
character. Indeed, it has been nationalist mobilization that in the past
enabled defense of democratic institutions from external and internal
aggression aimed at changing the political regime. It is no coincidence
that the United Kingdom never had, in the first half of the previous
century, authoritarian interruptions of its own democratic regime,

while authoritarian regimes became established in all the countries of continental Europe. However, in the post-Second World War period, while in western Europe nationalism has accepted the liberal constraints of the constitutional state, in eastern and central Europe nationalism's acceptance of the liberal constraints has been much more controversial. The form of this resistance needs to be addressed.

The Sovereignist Challenge of Illiberal Democracy

Owing to the unsatisfactory handling of the multiple crises of the 2010s, nationalism has thus resurfaced in the public attitudes of many countries of western Europe, justified by the criticism of scarcely legitimate and effective intergovernmental decisions (Tsoukalis 2016). At the same time, in the countries of eastern and central Europe, nationalism had never disappeared from the public debate. Indeed, it provided the conceptual, but also sentimental, model for the construction of the new post-Soviet identities of those countries. In the countries of the Visegrad Group (Poland, Hungary, the Czech Republic, and Slovakia), as in Romania and Bulgaria as well as in the Baltics, the end of the Cold War led to the drawing up of a new narrative, put forward both to internal and external public opinion, based on their self-absolution for the post-war authoritarian degeneration. The communist regimes that had organized those societies in the four decades following the Second World War were interpreted as (mainly) the expression of Moscow's domination over eastern and central Europe and not also as internal adherence to the anti-democratic values of that domination (as intellectual minorities of those countries continued to denounce). The domestic contribution to the formation of those regimes was therefore covered over, justifying a re-legitimization of post-Cold War nationalism as a sentiment without any authoritarian hangover. Thus, these countries were rebuilt, after 1989–1991, on nationalist bases, just when they were working to join a European integration process designed to undercut nationalist cultures (Kupchan 1995; Lacroix and Nicolaidis 2010: part IV; Sugar 1994). The result is that "the new generation of [eastern and central European] leaders experiences the constant pressure to adopt European norms and institutions as a humiliation and build their legitimacy around the idea of a national identity in opposition to Brussels" (Krastev 2017: 58). With the unaware superficiality of the political elites of western

Europe, the suspicion was buried that the rediscovered nationalism of the countries of eastern and central Europe had some responsibility in the tragedies of the first half of the twentieth century. There was no public reflection, in the countries of eastern and central Europe, on the characteristics of their nationalism and on the suitability of the latter with an integration process aimed toward a supranational outcome.

The more the crises have urged greater integration, the more integration has proved divisive as well as ineffective, and the stronger has been the convergence between populism and nationalism. Albeit with more modern language, the encounter between populism and nationalism has ended up creating different ideological combinations, all aiming, however, to promote the same politics of closure under the banner of sovereignism. That encounter has reproposed the distinction between "us" and "them," identifying the latter with a (presumed) cosmopolitan (thus rootless) community generated by European integration and the former with a (presumed) ethnically (thus rooted) national community. Albeit these ideological combinations are different, they nonetheless have a political trait in common: authoritarianism. Eastern and central European nationalism is moving toward illiberalism, justified by national constitutional tradition. In the name of their people (singular), leaders such as the Hungarian Viktor Orban, the Pole Jarosław Kaczyński, and the Rumanian Mihai Tudose have openly challenged the liberal restrictions of the constitutional state. In a speech given in July 2014 (at the twenty-fifth Bálványos Summer Free University and Student Camp), the Hungarian prime minister Viktor Orban said, "We must break with the liberal principles and methods of social organisation. (...) The liberal democracy was incapable of openly stating and committing the prevailing government, including the use of constitutional powers, to serving the interests of the nation. (...) The liberal democracy and the liberal Hungarian state did not protect community assets." In those countries, populism and nationalism have come together in the rejection of liberal principles (Mudde 2016). After decades of celebration by western jurists and politicians of European constitutional pluralism, considered to be the functional equivalent of an unnecessary supranational constitution, the diffusion of illiberal democracy in eastern and central Europe has shown the fallacy of European rhetoric. Constitutional pluralism is a double-edged concept. It aimed to make a supranational constitution unnecessary (Walker 2004; Weiler 2000); it ended up in disarming the EU relative to national constitutional deviations (Fabbrini F. 2015; Kelemen 2019). If liberal democracy is government of the *demos* within constitutional rules, illiberal democracy is government of a *demos*'s majority over constitutional rules. This populist nationalism has had no fear in implementing its illiberal program not only in Hungary but also in Poland (Bruszt 2017; Kelemen 2015). Indeed, the European Commission decided, in December 2017, to open up, for the first time, an infringement procedure (under Article 7[1] of the Treaty on European Union, TEU) against the Polish government for its reiterated violation of the principles of rule of law celebrated by Article 2 of the same treaty. Populist nationalism, with its connotations of political closure and anti-liberal elite, has not only become predominant in the countries of the Visegrad Goup (although challenged by groups of citizens of those countries), but it has also extended its influence on the larger area stemming from the Baltic states to Austria. In Italy, the party achieving the most votes in the elections of March 2018 (Five Star Movement) asserts in its statute the target of abandoning representative democracy constitutionalizing the principle of the binding mandate for members of the parliament.

However, contrary to what happened in the United Kingdom, the anti-Europeanism that aggregated nationalism and populism in eastern and central Europe has not claimed the dismantling of the integration project. This is also true for the Scandinavian countries that could not guarantee their standard of living without being part of the EU single market. The British idea of self-sufficiency, derived from the imperial experience of the country, cannot be confused with the sovereignism claimed by nationalists and populists in Europe. It seems likely, though, that in the United Kingdom the idea of self-sufficiency will be dramatically challenged by the post-Brexit realities. In particular, the countries of eastern and central Europe need the economic support and geo-strategic coverage from being part of the EU. Again, as the Hungarian prime minister Viktor Orban said at the Conference of the European People's Party (held in Valletta, Malta, on March 30, 2017), "We are grateful to God for being able to re-join Europe and being able to become members of the European Union." Indeed, being part of the European People's Party, Viktor Orban and his party (Fidesz) have been able to pursue their illiberal policies without triggering the Commission's reaction, as happened with Poland. The eleven Fidesz seats in the 2014–2019 European Parliament were important for guaranteeing the majority supporting the *Spizenkandidat* of the European People's Party, Jean-Claude Juncker, as president of the Commission, which was not the case for the Polish Law and Justice governing party, whose members in the European Parliament were affiliated with the quite marginal group of the European Conservatives and Reformists (ECR). Thus, rather than secede from the EU, the sovereignist governments are claiming more decision-making autonomy from the EU, particularly in the issues (such as migration) considered crucial by the governing party. The affirmation of national sovereignty, by those countries, does not imply the return to the national sovereignties of the pre-Second War World period. The exit from the EU is not (for now) the model for the European nationalists and populists.

Motivated by the noble desire to peacefully reconcile the whole continent, the EU enlargement to the eastern and central European countries (in 2005 and 2007) was pursued by the western political elites without considering the deep nationalist culture that exists in those countries. Those elites ended up confusing their desires with reality. This anti-realist tendency to look at politics through a normative lens is still in full force in Brussels, where (for example) the negotiations with Montenegro and Serbia to join the EU continue undisturbed, despite the openly nationalist sentiment of those countries. Turkey was even promised that negotiations for it to join the EU would be reopened, on the condition that it retain millions of Syrian refugees within its territory. Plausibly, for those accepting that deal, the latter was a necessary short-term prize to pay for keeping Angela Merkel at the helm of German government (as, indeed, happened), but the long-term consequences of the deal might result in something that is barely manageable (Megan and Kelemen 2016). Despite the rhetoric on the vanishing of the borders between western and eastern Europe, despite the good intentions on the need to heal the divisions of the Cold War, and despite the naive illusion that nationalism is a sentiment of the past, the multiple crises of the second decade of the twenty-first century have brought sovereignism as a governing force in eastern and central Europe and as a very influential force in western and southern Europe (a force that arrived in power in Italy). Prisoners of the normative cage according to which the EU *should* include all the states of Europe, EU elites could not devise any alternative perspective, particularly one based on the distinction between economic and political integration – a distinction that has now imposed itself in the European agenda.

Sovereignism and Economic Integration

It is difficult to understand the strength, not only the persistence, of nationalism without considering the growing interdependence brought by the process of integration. Pressured by the necessity to deal with the multiple crises of the 2010s, interdependence has arrived to touch on crucial prerogatives of EU member states. This impact has triggered different reactions in different member states according to the view that historically inspired the relation of each of them with the process of integration. Those different reactions epitomized the differing trajectories followed by the EU member states in building their nation state and its subsequent democratization. For a group of western European countries (located geographically on the periphery of Europe, in the British Isles and Scandinavia) the integration process should have a purely economic significance. For these countries, the perspective for integration is, and continues to be, that of building and making operative a continental market regime, an "economic community" (which, after all, the EU was called in 1973, when the United Kingdom, Denmark, and Ireland joined). Moreover, these countries decided to join the EU after the failure of the alternative integration project, the European Free Trade Association (EFTA), which was set up in 1960 and of which they were members (together with Iceland, Liechtenstein, Norway, and Switzerland). The EFTA was (and continues to be) a project of exclusively economic cooperation. Since joining the EU, the United Kingdom has been the most coherent proponent of this vision of integration, based on a combination of transnational economic cooperation and preservation of national (parliamentary) sovereignty. The logic of voluntary cooperation, although institutionalized through intergovernmental coordination, is acceptable as long as it prevents the possibility of undermining national (parliamentary) sovereignty.

To these countries were added, considerably increasing the influence of the economic integration's coalition, the countries of eastern and central Europe that had joined the EU with the enlargements of 2005 and 2007. These countries, which had just won back their national sovereignty with the end of the Cold War, adhered to the integration process for geo-economic, not political, assessments. For them, it meant being part not only of an organization that would favor their economic growth (as then happened), but also of an organization that would anchor them to the West (also symbolically). Indeed, for these prior countries, it was more important to have participation in NATO than in the EU. The anchoring was interpreted as alliance more than integration, because their restored national sovereignty could not be thrown into doubt again, albeit this time by a supranational democratic organization. Hence the contradictory relationship that these countries have maintained with the EU. On the one hand, participation in the latter has protected them from any hegemonic desire of their long-time enemy (Russia). On the other hand, however, such participation has weakened the national sovereignty that they have just won back. This contradiction has ended up in triggering, in those countries, a growing problematic attitude toward the EU. In fact, they entered the latter with a primarily economic interpretation of the integration process, as if they had to participate in an organization of regional economic cooperation, and they found themselves entrapped in an extended net of supranational regulations. What the Brussels authorities perceived as an instrumental attitude of those countries toward the EU, from those countries' perspective it was (and is) the opposite, with the EU intruding on their regained sovereignty. It would be the same perspective for the other countries (i.e., the Balkan states) that are queuing up to join the EU. For the countries of eastern and central Europe, being part of the EU was, and is, a condition to promote their economic growth and to guarantee their geo-strategic security, but certainly not to constrain their regained national sovereignty. The multiple crises of the 2010s have shown that there is a very broad area of member states of the EU, in the peninsular north and east of the continent (apart from the United Kingdom) that is solely interested in transnational economic cooperation and not in political integration.

After all, for the countries of the islands and peninsulas of the north (and for the United Kingdom particularly), the nation state (and its ideology: nationalism) has been an instrument to defend democracy, not to bury it, as happened in the countries of western continental Europe, hence the deliberate and constant action of these countries (and the United Kingdom particularly) to slow down the integration process, especially in policy sectors considered crucial for the nation state (such as defense and foreign policy). For them, the integration process must not undermine the institutions and the powers of the nation state, and thus the role as decision-maker of last resort for the national parliament and its government. Sovereignty means this: having the power to have the final word on disputed issues. For these countries, democracy, if interpreted as citizens' capability of exercising control over public choices, can prosper only in the nation state. The latter is the natural condition of democratic politics, because it protects and limits such a system through its juridical and administrative institutions. The nation state not only is a configuration of institutional power, but also is the basic source of identification for citizens. The democratic state is the sum of traditions, practices, and values that cannot be weakened by supranational integration processes. Outside of the confines of the nation state there can be, and there must be, cooperation and even coordination, but not integration (pooling, but not sharing, national sovereignties). There can be a single market (such as that promoted by the Single European Act of 1986, which the United Kingdom pushed for), but not supranational politics.

Given the inevitable drive to the institutional deepening of the EU (particularly after the 1990 German reunification and the 1992 Treaty of Maastricht), these countries have asked for and obtained a series of opt-outs from the most integrating policies and regimes, starting with the Eurozone that manages the common currency. The Lisbon Treaty of 2009 then formalized the existence of those opt-outs. Before Brexit, the United Kingdom had been able to benefit from a truly special regime of exemptions. Moreover, for preventing the possibility of Brexit, the then British prime minister, David Cameron, and the president of the European Council, Donald Tusk, signed an agreement, in February 2016, which recognized further exemptions for the country. The agreement exempted the country from the need to pursue the (symbolic but highly political) aim of an "ever closer union," which from the 1957 Treaties of Rome to the 2009 Lisbon Treaty epitomized the political purpose of the integration process. The agreement between Cameron and Tusk formally recognized that, for the United Kingdom (and, implicitly, for the countries that identified themselves in its approach), the EU was and is a purely economic project. The agreement says (European Council 2016: 9–10), "The Treaties allow an evolution towards a deeper degree of integration among the Member States that share such a vision of their common future, without this applying to other Member States. It is recognized that the United Kingdom, in the light of the specific situation it has under the Treaties, is not committed to further political integration into the European Union." In a previous paragraph, it significantly said that "references in the Treaties and their preambles to the process of creating an ever closer union among the peoples of Europe are primarily intended to signal that the Union's aim is to promote trust and understanding among peoples living in open and democratic societies sharing a common heritage of universal values. They are not an equivalent to the objective of political integration." This statement contradicted a long-established understanding of the clause and irritated several political leaders (in the European Commission, the European Parliament, and Eurozone member states).

Even if pursued doggedly, the economic vision of integration has been accompanied by significant ambiguity. Neither the old nor new countries that assert the primacy of national sovereignty have ever tried to specify what their interpretation implies for the single market. The latter is indeed much more than a customs union or regional economic area, such as that sought by various intergovernmental organizations (e.g., the North American Free Trade Agreement [NAFTA] and the *Mercado Común del Sur* [MERCOSUR] in the Americas, or the Association of Southeast Asian Nations [ASEAN] and the Asia-Pacific Economic Cooperation [APEC] in Asia; Fabbrini 2015a: ch. 4). The single market could not function without effective supranational administrative and legal institutions, such as the European Court of Justice (which is needed to resolve disputes between the legislations of the states) and the Commission (which is needed to promote policy solutions not conditioned by national interests). Such a continental market would also need a legislature (representative of national governments and citizens) authorized to approve provisions needed to make it work. To use the language of Brussels functionaries, the former institutions serve to eliminate the obstacles that hinder the working of a single market (negative integration), the latter instead serve to substitute the national legislations with common supranational rules (positive integration).

The agreement (between Tusk and Cameron) left unresolved the question of whether a single market can function based mainly on voluntary mechanisms of transnational cooperation or it requires a more compelling mechanism of supranational regulation. Incapable of clarifying to themselves what their vision of the single market is, the national leaders of the economic integration's coalition have continued to play a reactive rather than a proactive game. The western/northern national leaders have specialized in the opt-out game, the eastern and central national leaders have instead pursued a free-riding game, taking what suits them (financing from the structural funds program) and rejecting what doesn't (the allocation to them of a share of political refugees). One might add that the free-riding countries are pursuing a strategy of unofficial nullification of those EU decisions considered undesirable by the incumbent governments.

The view of sovereignists was made even more ambiguous by the unsuccessful experience of Brexit. Brexit shows the difficulty of balancing national sovereignty and interdependence *outside* of the EU, but it leaves unsettled the question of how to balance national sovereignty and interdependence *within* the EU. The United Kingdom arrived not only politically unprepared for secession, but above all it met insurmountable hurdles in defining a plausible post-secession strategy. The British elites did not even know who had the power to start the separation procedure in the case of Brexit, the Parliament or the government, with the outcome that the question was decided by the judiciary (a paradox for a democracy that has always exalted the sovereignty of its own Parliament, to the extent that it still does not have a written constitution). Therefore, the decision was made to delay for nine months (after the referendum) the triggering of Art. 50 of the Lisbon Treaty (which regulates the secession of a member state from the EU). In addition, because the negotiation covers a considerable number of commercial matters, it was acknowledged by British political authorities that effective secession from the EU would take more than two years (as Art. 50 envisages). Finally, although the United Kingdom will have to formally leave the EU on March 29, 2019, British and European negotiators reached an agreement that was highly contested in London. As expected by several scholars (Fabbrini F. 2017), Brexit has made British politics chaotic. For the sovereignists, the Brexit experience is tantamount to a political shock (Fabbrini F. 2017) or a political drama (Craig 2017). It showed not only how unprepared were the British elites, long considered a model of political competence (thus unmasking the presumption of their cultural superiority, particularly toward the elites of southern Europe), but also how unfeasible and exacting might be the choice to exit the single market. The economic perspective of integration is powerful as an evocation but weak as a program. Let's now consider the alternative position, the political vision of integration expressed by the clause of an "ever closer union."

Europeanism and Political Integration

The successful mobilization of sovereignist forces has challenged the pro-EU parties and leaders. The political interpretation of the process of integration has characterized mainly western continental European countries. In the latter countries, nationalism could not be the source of their post-war reconstruction. It was nationalism that provided the ideology and incited the mobilization aimed at bringing down democratic (or, in any case, liberal) institutions between the two world wars of the last century. It is no coincidence that it was the countries of continental western Europe that started, in the second half of the previous century, the process of supranational integration to build up stronger antibodies to resist the nationalistic virus that previously and repeatedly infected them. The countries of western continental Europe (such as Germany, France, and Italy), which contributed to three European civil wars in less than a century, could not permit themselves a purely economic vision of the integration process (Lacroix and Nicolaidis 2010). After the rejection of the project for a European Defence Community by the French parliament in 1954, these countries turned to economic integration with the aim, however, of creating the conditions for a future political integration. In these countries, the nation state (and its ideology: nationalism) was discredited by its responsibility in opening the door to totalitarian regimes. Integration was seen, by the new political elites that took hold after the Second World War, as the response to the historic weakness of the liberal antibodies of their national societies. For this reason, integration took on a decidedly political aspect. For such post-war leaders, it was a question of transforming the international relations between European states into domestic relations of a supranational organization. The Second World War called definitively into question the Newtonian idea that rivalry between nation states could be kept at bay through the impersonal mechanism of balancing their power. It is in this context that the idea and the need of a politically united Europe developed, particularly in the two countries (France and West Germany) that historically embodied the intra-European rivalry. West German and French elites shared a political view of the "ever closer union" clause, although they differed for quite a while in interpreting it (thus converging after the 1990 German reunification). Let's look more closely at the nature of the political view of integration.

In West Germany (formally, the Federal Republic of Germany, or *Bundesrepublik Deutschland*), the radical de-legitimization of the nation state led to its cultural reworking toward a constitutional patriotism rooted in European political unity. The nation (as an ideological concept) was replaced by the homeland (as an empirical reality), a homeland protected by a new constitution (*Grundgesetz*). In West Germany, this reconstruction was of a titanic nature. In modern history, there have been no cases of collective self-analysis comparable with the experience of post-war West Germany (specifically starting at the end of the 1960s) (Judt 2005). It was self-analysis aimed at reinventing the identity of the people of West Germany on the basis of the explicit recognition of their own dramatic historical responsibilities (in the Holocaust of the Jews and in the two world wars). Nothing of the kind has happened in other European countries (Italy and Austria), which were allies of Germany during those tragedies (setting aside non-European countries such as Japan, which still today struggle to come to terms with their actions in the Second World War). In acknowledging their historical responsibilities, West German elites brought to the post-war construction of the European integration's project the contribution of their federal experience of a parliamentary state, given its success in consolidating the country's democracy.

The efforts of the West German post-war elites to promote public reflection on Germany's responsibilities seemed, however, to have stalled after the reunification in October 1990. That reunification involved the absorption of a genuine state (the German Democratic Republic, or *Deutsche Demokratische Republik*, with a population of almost 17 million) into the Federal Republic of Germany. Overnight, the former became the eastern part of the latter, in the form of five new *Länder* (Brandenburg, Mecklenburg-Vorpommern, Saxony, Saxony-Anhalt, and Thuringia) and the new city-state of Berlin (which was previously divided into western and eastern halves). This reunification was not accompanied (either before or, above all, after) by an equivalent reflection on the historical responsibilities of German nationalism by East Germany (Jarausch 1994). Indeed, the latter's citizens came to perceive themselves as victims of the reunification, giving rise in the new *Länder* to nationalist sentiment critical of the traditional

Europeanism of West Germany. This cultural change was epitomized by the growing electoral success of the nationalist party of *Alternative für Deutschland* particularly in the eastern *Länder,* as testified by the *Bundestag* election of September 2017. The fact is that the reunified Germany is no longer the same country that contributed to the initiation and development of the European integration process. For both its political and technocratic elites (just think of the members of its constitutional court, *Bundesverfassungsgericht,* or the governors of its central bank, *Deutsche Bundesbank*), Germany is now a country like the others, a country that must no longer fear pursuing its national interest or affirming its national identity (Bulmer and Paterson 2010). Indeed, those elites gradually discovered the benefits of an intergovernmental EU wherein the German government can play a powerful role in defending or promoting German interests.

The parliamentary/supranational view on the integration process has thus gradually (and silently) become an intergovernmental one, particularly in policy fields of crucial salience for domestic public opinion (as economic policy). Albeit kept in check by the leaders of the biggest political parties, nationalism has not only returned to being a legitimate sentiment, but it has also obscured the traditional supranational/parliamentary view of Europe constructed by post-war German ruling elites. Germany is no longer prisoner to its sense of guilt and is seen by its European partners as a country fully legitimated by its extraordinary results (in terms of economic growth and constitutional stability) achieved after the Second World War. However, in times of crises in the economy or with immigration, this renewed national pride has stoked a position of closure toward the equally legitimate interests of other countries (particularly southern European, such as Greece), with the result that the necessary reconciliation with its own national identity ended up creating unnecessary divisions with the national identities of other European countries. Thus, the rediscovery of its own national identity has led German elites not to become anti-Europeanist, but their Europeanism has acquired an intergovernmental character. German support for the integration process has come to be justified by the advantages (above all economic) that it provides to the country, rather than by moral or historical considerations, an advantage that can be secured only through a direct involvement of the government in the EU decision-making process. Hence, the preference of post-unification German governments for the intergovernmental rather than supranational approach (promoted instead by pre-unification German governments), which valorizes its economic weight, its judicial culture, and its political influence.

Although a united Europe continues to represent the main political horizon for mainstream German elites (Bulmer 2014), nonetheless they have changed their idea on the form the integration's project should take. Germany continues to need Europe, but a Europe led by national governments more than by supranational/parliamentary institutions. In a Europe of national governments, Germany can play a central political role. One example among many is the following: the preparation of the informal European Council held in Bratislava on September 16, 2016. It was the first meeting between heads of national government after the British referendum and the first meeting without the British prime minister. Who took the initiative to prepare that meeting? According to the treaties, it fell to Donald Tusk (president of the European Council) and Jean-Claude Juncker (president of the Commission), operating from Brussels as the base for European institutions. But that is not what happened. The initiative was instead taken by the German chancellor, Angela Merkel. In the week preceding the meeting, she met the leaders of separate groups of countries (close in regional terms) – first Italy and France, and then the Baltic countries, followed by the Visegrad Group (the Czech Republic, Poland, Slovakia, and Hungary), the heads of government of northern Europe (Finland, Sweden, Denmark, and the Netherlands), and finally ending with the leaders of central Europe (Austria, Bulgaria, Croatia, and Slovenia). The only leaders whom Merkel did not meet were those of southern Europe (Spain, Portugal, Greece, Cyprus, and Malta). Probably, in the minds of the German leadership, their representation was subcontracted to the Italian and French leaders. On that occasion, Merkel divided the EU into regional areas, or sub-continental sections, each identified by specific requests (the Baltics wanted security, Visegrad and central Europe did not want refugees, northern Europeans wanted rigor, and southern Europeans wanted flexibility). The German government instead considered it was the only one following a general agenda, although its action aimed to affirm its own national interests. The German government acted as the network that holds the other states together, the hub holding the spokes of the wheel, in a system in which the political divisions between governments of left and right count increasingly less, while divisions of interests between states and regional areas count increasingly more. By balancing one area with another, the German leadership thus transferred the center of political decision-making from Brussels to Berlin. Maybe reluctantly (Bulmer and Paterson 2013), Germany has installed itself at the center of a union of national governments, a union administratively centralized as an organization with statehood's properties.

The aim of building an "ever closer union" was much more contrasted in France. That aim, however, came to be shared by mainstream political elites, although it was justified by the narrative stressing the politically hegemonic role the country played in setting up European common institutions reflecting French principles and values. Sitting on the winners' side at the end of the Second World War, French (but also British) elites were reluctant to acknowledge their country's responsibilities in the massacres committed during their tenure as colonial and imperial powers (Nicolaidis, Sèbe, and Maas 2015). Indeed, for a long time, the same Vichy experience (1940–1944) was interpreted by the French post-war political and intellectual elites as the occupation of the country by Nazi Germany and not also as the adherence of many French citizens and political elites to the goals being pursued by Nazi Germany (Jackson 2003). French national identity has remained politically ambiguous, oscillating between the defense of the nation state and the exaltation of a European state.

The German reunification of October 1990 altered the structural symmetry between the two countries. The French elites tried to tame, with the 1992 Maastricht Treaty, that alteration through the institutionalization of an intergovernmental model for deciding policies considered strategic. Because that model was based on voluntary coordination, which means unanimity in making decisions, French governments presumed to have a tool for controlling German power. For the two decades after Maastricht, France was indeed able to check Germany, because the latter had to shoulder the social and economic costs of its national reunification. The German reforms of the 2000s created, however, the conditions for the recovery of the country. After those reforms (known as Agenda 2010, although the Hartz reforms of the labor market were also crucial), Germany was no longer the "sick man of Europe." The euro crisis, begun 2009–2010, found Germany in a better economic condition than France. The following multiple crises again altered the power relations between the two countries, establishing the preeminence of a reformed Germany over an unreformed France. Indeed, with the 1990 reunification of Germany, France gradually lost its central position in European politics (and geography). The euro crisis highlighted the fact that France can no longer counterbalance Germany, even within the intergovernmental deliberation. During the euro crisis, the Franco-German engine of integration broke down, leaving Germany as the undisputed leader of the Eurozone. It was a worrying systemic development because, in the past, the divergences between France and Germany had allowed the "multilateralization" of the integration process. The smallest states could see themselves in one or another position, allowed to play an autonomous role for the purposes of mediation between the two countries. Having justified its support for European integration on the basis of the systemic necessity to keep Germany in check, France lost its way when it had to acknowledge that Germany no longer needed France's tutorship and warranty to be politically legitimate.

From the referendum on the Treaty of Maastricht of 1992 to the 2017 election of Emmanuel Macron to the French presidency, French elites (Gaullist and socialist, as they alternated in power) were unable to devise a new narrative of the relationship of their country with Europe (Lacroix 2010). Although the interpretation of the EU as France writ large was disproved by the facts, nonetheless those elites refused to acknowledge that European integration required a substantial revision of the country's vision on European integration. Those elites maintained the ambiguity of a country forced to advance integration but fearing that this might call its historic identity into question. In this way, it maintained a rich soil that encouraged the growth of a radically nationalist right wing (represented by the *Front National*, renamed the *Rassemblement National* in 2018), which became the leading party of the country in the elections for the European Parliament in May 2014 and whose leader (Marine Le Pen) was the main adversary of Emmanuel Macron in the 2017 presidential elections (getting more than a third of the votes). France's identity crisis enabled a drastic diminution, during the financial crisis, of the multilateral character of the Eurozone. The latter, which was constructed on intergovernmental bases at France's own insistence to balance Germany's new strength, ended up being increasingly hierarchical and blinkered. The new asymmetry between the two countries left Germany without a significant balancing weight. Moreover, during those multiple crises, French elites did not want to promote a new institutional setting within which to envelop German power. During the euro crisis, the Eurozone continued to speak German, in the sense that Germany defined the problems and the solutions for the Eurozone's preservation.

The arrival of Emmanuel Macron at the Élysée Palace in May 2017 reversed the subordinate role of France toward Germany, because the new presidency came to intersect with the German stalemate in forming a government after the *Bundestag* elections of September 24, 2017. Moreover, from the beginning of his tenure, the French president has elaborated a new narrative on European integration (and on the role France should play in it). Two days after the German elections, the French president gave his (widely considered) historical speech at the Sorbonne, where he delineated a new French vision of Europe and the Eurozone. At the same time, contradicting the previous French submission to the German ordo-liberal orthodoxy, Macron also advanced a proposal for a substantial reform of the Eurozone through the creation of an independent budget run by a European minister of finance. The new French position has restored the political interpretation of the "ever closer union" perspective, freeing it from the cage where it was imprisoned by the *realpolitik* of Donald Tusk (when he made the deal with the then British prime minister David Cameron). However, although much more innovative and audacious than those advanced in the past, the new French position seems to have preserved a statist ambiguity or tone on a sovereign Europe. In sum, both the German and the French political views of integration have a centralizing bias as if the "ever closer union" means the construction of a European polity superseding the national.

Conclusion

In many EU member states, there has been a strengthening of the alliance between nationalism and populism, although with different impacts in the west and the east (plus the British Isles and the Scandinavian peninsula). Nationalism has increased its strength and legitimacy allying with the populist critique of the EU, a critique that has assumed the EU to be an organization controlled by technocratic elites. This mobilization was conducted on behalf of a population allegedly ignored by those very technocratic elites and certainly penalized by the integration process. The combination of nationalism and populism has led to sovereignism as a public philosophy claiming the compatibility between national sovereignty and economic integration. Contrary to the British interpretation of sovereignty, in fact, the sovereignist elites of the other European countries have claimed the possibility of accommodating the preservation of national sovereignty with the functioning of a single market. Although the sovereignist mobilization has been different from country to country (and from regional areas to others), it has shown that there is a basic distinction between the economic view of integration (particularly strong in eastern and central Europe) and the political view (traditionally shared by western continental European leaders and community institutions' representatives).

The division between sovereignism and Europeanism, triggered by the multiple crises of the 2010s, reflects the different perspectives on integration characterizing the EU member states. Those visions were not the result of contingent electoral interests but rather the expression of deeper national interpretations of sovereignty and democracy. The states participating in the integration process have continued to have differently interpreted the relationship between national sovereignty and supranational authority, just as they have differently interpreted the role of national democratic institutions compared with supranational institutions. Contingent electoral changes have mitigated those views, but they could not silence them. These different interpretations of the integration process have remained within the same legal and institutional framework as long as that process favored all its participants. However, when the multiple crises and their intergovernmental governance started to generate redistributive effects, those different views have powerfully reemerged. The multiple crises of the 2010s and the 2016 Brexit have ended up in calling into question the coexistence of the economic vision (with its sovereignist bias) and the political visions (with its Europeanist bias) of integration within the same legal framework.

This chapter has thus discussed the backbone of two views, the idea of economic integration backing sovereignist forces and the idea of political integration backing Europeanist forces, highlighting their ambiguities. It is not clear (to sovereignists) how to combine a single market with national sovereignties, nor is it clear (to Europeanists) how to combine a European democracy with the democracy of nation states. If the economic vision of integration is ambiguous regarding the role of supranational institutions for making the single market function, the political vision of integration continues to be unambiguous regarding the role of national democracies in its European sovereignty. It is now necessary to deepen the analysis of the political view of integration, discussing both its parliamentary and intergovernmental versions (as they have been alternatively entertained by western continental European elites), with the aim of investigating whether an anti-statist vision of political integration is (at least theoretically) possible.

4 | From Statist to Federal Political Union

Introduction

The statist model is a formidable cognitive (as well as political) limitation on the future of Europe. In Europe, the political view of integration continues to be one with the idea of state. Recall the clause "ever closer union," which evokes a centralizing logic that was a historically proper process of state building. This is the outcome of an analytical misunderstanding of federalism, a theory associated with statehood (and thus refused by those opposing the latter as the EU's outcome). As Mény (2014: 1350) observed, "A federation is not by itself a centralised system." By not distinguishing between federalism by disaggregation and federalism by aggregation, the European political culture has ended up associating federalism with both a state and a government. Only by dissociating federalism from the state and from its government is it possible to put the future of Europe on realistic bases. If the federal state is the outcome of the disaggregation of a previously unitary unit, the outcome of the aggregation of states that were previously separated is unlikely to give rise to a federal state. Because the aggregation generally consists of states that are asymmetric on a demographic level and distinct in terms of national identities, it is understandable that those states aim to form a *union* which is neither supported by a state organization higher than they are nor governed by an institution with final decision-making power which can control them (Fabbrini 2017a).

This is what happened on the empirical level, if we consider the only two successful cases of federalism by aggregation within the family of consolidated democracies, i.e., the US and Switzerland. Both came into being as federal unions with a vertical separation of powers; they then consolidated with a weak central setup, and they equipped themselves with a system of government with horizontal separation between the

87

institutions of the federal center. Both are systems with fragmented or divided sovereignty. An institutional strategy aims to protect the multiple identities by which they are constructed. For this reason, it is necessary to redefine the aggregation's model among the European states, replacing the statist logic with a union's perspective. This chapter is organized as follows: First, it discusses the two main political perspectives on integration (the parliamentary and the intergovernmental) to show their intrinsic statist logic. Second, it moves beyond the statist paradigm, delineating the intellectual features of the federal union, based on multiple separation of powers. Third, it focuses on the US experience of building a successful federal union out of the aggregation of previously independent states (an experience thus followed by Switzerland). The aim of the discussion is to identify the method used by the US constitutional founders, not to delineate a model the EU should imitate, a method finalized to create "a sovereign union of sovereign states." Fourth, that method is thus applied to solve the governance's puzzle of the EU.

The Statist Paradigms: Parliamentary and Intergovernmental

The first political perspective of integration can be defined as that of the federal state of a parliamentary type. This perspective has been supported steadily by the Italian political elites and, up until the 1990s, by the German political elites – i.e., by the ruling elites of the two countries that had the greatest need to re-legitimize themselves on the international and European levels. This perspective accompanied the integration process from the start and culminated in the direct election of the members of the European Parliament in 1979 (thus formalized by the "Draft Treaty establishing the European Union" approved by the European Parliament in 1984 on the initiative of Altiero Spinelli, then a member of that legislature). The enlargement of the EU to include Spain and Portugal in 1986 helped strengthen the perspective of federal parliamentarism, seen by the elites of the countries emerging from authoritarianism as the supranational safeguard for the newborn national democracies. This perspective then reached its peak in the Convention to draw up a Constitutional Treaty for the EU held in Brussels between 2002 and 2003. After the defeat of the Constitutional Treaty in the popular referendum held in France and the Netherlands in 2005, federal parliamentarism was then relaunched by the main political parties, with the proposal of running the 2014 and 2019 elections to the European Parliament with a a *Spitzenkandidat* for each party list.

For the main parties of the European Parliament (the Christian Democrats, the Social Democrats, and the Liberal Democrats), the parliamentary election of the president of the Commission represents the necessary condition to reduce the EU's democratic deficit. With the strategy of the *Spitzenkandidaten*, an attempt was made to promote democratization as the parliamentarization of the EU (Christiansen 2016). The *Spitzenkandidaten*'s logic reflects the important, if not hegemonic, role played historically by German parliamentarians, for a long time the largest national parliamentary delegations in the European Parliament's two main groups (the Christian Democrats and the Socialist Democrats). Those parliamentarians have conveyed a federal vision derived from their national experience. Through the German parliamentarians, a political culture has spread in the European Parliament that has taken the parliamentary federal state as the inevitable and necessary outcome of the integration process, a federal state organized in accordance with the criteria of close cooperation or, better, fusion among both the horizontal and vertical institutions of decision-making. The very configuration of the Council of Ministers, as representing the governments of the member states, refers to the experience of the German senate, or *Bundesrat*, which is made up of representatives of the governments of the *Länder*.

The nation state, according to parliamentarists, can be overcome by and through a post-national parliamentary system (Rittberger 2005), through the formation of a federal European state, equipped with authority and legitimacy superior to those of the nation states constituting it, i.e., a federal state based on a bicameral parliament in accordance with the model successfully tried by post-war federal Germany. Certainly, parliamentarists acknowledge the importance of the Council of Ministers as the institution representing national governments; however, from the parliamentarist perspective it is the European Parliament that has been the real depositary of the EU's democratic legitimacy (as is the case of the *Bundestag* in the German experience). The Commission must exercise the role of European government, with the European Parliament and the Council of Ministers operating in accordance with the logic of a legislature that represents both citizens (the former) and governments (the latter) (Hix 2008). This is the case of the German *Bundestag* and *Bundesrat* (with the former representing the citizens and the latter the country's *Länder* or, better, their executives), where, however, the source of the government's political legitimacy resides in the former and not in the latter chamber.

Parliamentary federal states, in fact, are politically centralized and based on a system of government that entrusts to a single chamber (the popularly elected chamber) the duty of expressing political confidence or no-confidence in the government. This is possible because there is both a reasonable demographic balance between the territorial units and a sufficient homogeneity in their political culture. Such is the case in Germany, which is, according to Scharpf (2008: 510), a "federal state with a unitary political culture. It is a federal state with parliamentary governments at the national level [where] there are no politically salient territorial cleavages defined by ethnic, linguistic, or religious divisions, and no popular demands for regional autonomy." In parliamentary federal states, the parties themselves aggregate the political differences in all the units of the territorial system. Parliamentary federal states do not aggregate nation states that are consistently dissimilar in terms of size and national identity, but (demographically) comparable territorial units and (politically) homogeneous social communities. Indeed, in those federal states (such as Canada) where territorial national identities have become established (such as Quebec), the parliamentary model struggles to operate (Fossum and Menéndez 2011). The same happened in Belgium, in Spain, and in the post-devolution United Kingdom, once the identity's radicalization of their distinct linguistic communities exploded. The parliamentary model can function only where there are no significant demographic asymmetries and deep national identity differences between the territorial units of the federation.

It can be said that the European parliamentarists have simply enlarged the geographical dimensions of the concepts (state and democracy) that make up European political modernity, thinking to have thus solved the political dilemmas intrinsic to these concepts if transferred on a supranational scale. Even if comparative politics scholars (such as Lijphart 1999) interpreted the EU as a federal state in the making, whose democratic functioning could be linked to the ideal-type of consensual democracy typical of small European countries with identity divisions (such as Luxembourg, Belgium, Austria, the Netherlands, and Switzerland), it is unlikely that the EU will become a parliamentary federal state. The EU arises from the aggregation of nationally distinct and demographically asymmetric states that would resist their superseding by a superior political entity. Aggregation of states would have difficulties in accommodating the centralization of decision-making through one form or another of the fusion of executive and legislative powers and overlapping between levels of government. It is necessary to recognize that parliamentary government would favor the larger states at the detriment of the smaller ones (because of their different representation in the legislature). Even if federal states have institutionalized intergovernmental relations (formally in Germany in the *Bundesrat*, informally in Canada through the First Ministers' Conference), nonetheless they have not institutionalized the intergovernmental logic (Fabbrini 2017b). The political decisions of the two federal states (Germany and Canada) are decided by the respective governments on the basis of the political confidence that connects each of them to the majority of the popularly elected chamber (the *Bundestag* in the former, the House of Commons in the latter). Despite the popularity of this perspective, nonetheless it has not managed to transform the EU into a parliamentary federal state.

The parliamentarist vision has been challenged by an equally political, but equally statist, perspective, the intergovernmental perspective (whose constitutional roots are in the 1992 Maastricht Treaty). It is political, because it recognizes the need for greater European integration, taking its distance from the economic vision that interprets integrated Europe as the regime of the only single market. Indeed, the logic of the intergovernmental union aims at regulating at the suprastate level the decision on those policies traditionally at the core of state power at the national level. It is statist, because, in assuming national governments are the key players in European governance, it forces them to interact within a centralized framework. The aim is to avoid moral hazard, i.e., the behavior through which one government could off-load on to another the costs of its expediencies. It is important to note that intergovernmentalism cannot be confounded with sovereignism. The reasons why this perspective has taken hold derive from the combination of national views (in particular, the French traditional preference for executive power; Lacroix 2010) and national interests (in particular, the German since the unification of the country in 1990; Muller 2010). This vision has promoted an idea of integration as a process with political ends, controlled, however, by national governments that coordinate themselves within the intergovernmental bodies institutionalized in Brussels. An intergovernmental union has therefore become mainly established in the Eurozone, giving life to institutions with their own specific decision-making role (such as the Euro Summit of the heads of government and the Eurogroup of economic and finance ministers) (Puetter 2014).

In this perspective, the European Parliament is a redundant institution, while the Commission and the European Court of Justice are institutions that can help resolve the problems of collective action. Decision-making powers are (and must remain) in the hands of the national leaders and ministers. The development of the 2015 Greek crisis provided a striking example of the logic of this model. That crisis was managed by the heads of government (at the meetings of the Euro Summit), the decisions of which were then implemented by supranational institutions such as the Commission (in collaboration with a non-European financial institution, the International Monetary Fund) and thus by national legislatures. In that crisis, the European Parliament did not play any significant role, while that role was exercised by some national parliaments (starting with the *Bundestag*). Indeed, because the financial aid to Greece consisted of financial transfers from the countries of the Eurozone, it was inevitable that the final decision on the possibility of realizing these transfers was made by the national parliaments of the largest creditor countries, Germany in particular. The intergovernmental union, created to reconcile national democracy with the supranational governance of strategic policies, ended up doing the opposite. It led to an increasingly centralized Eurozone, within which decisions were inevitably made under the impulse of the strongest states that were also the creditor states, in the absence of significant supranational parliamentary control.

The administrative centralization that has taken place within the Eurozone is unparalleled in any other democratic unions of states. According to Federico Fabbrini (2016: 15), "The new EU constitutional architecture of economic governance has become characterized by greater centralization, greater judicialization, and greater asymmetry between states than what occurs in a fully fledged federal regime with all-powerful judicial review like the US." This regulatory centralization has assumed that all member states might (or even should) adopt the same model of political economy, converging toward a pattern of economic organization and interest representation considered neutral but indeed derived from that institutionalized in the countries of northern Europe (Schelkle 2017). This uniformity's thrust had, however, dramatic effects on interstate relations. Centralizing economic policy decisions aimed to align national policies around a standard pattern had the effect of increasing interstate divisions and infrastate contestation. While the northern states benefited from the Eurozone's policies, the southern states had to pay very high social costs because of the latter. The centralization of the decision-making process (whatever form it takes, judicial or administrative) and the link between national and European politics (where national leaders make European decisions and the latter affect the former) epitomize the statist logic of the intergovernmental interpretation of the "ever closer union." Behind the intergovernmental union, there is the idea that the Eurozone can consolidate only if supported by non-negotiable central rules through which to generate economic convergence and cultural uniformity between the states that are part of it – an economic convergence that might be encumbered by political discretion. Indeed, the opposite should have been followed. As argued powerfully by Schelkle (2017: 311), "The risk-sharing perspective on international cooperation suggests that it is imperative for the pool to maintain the diversity it has. Existing arrangements must nurture diversity for its own sake but also in order to keep up the rationale for collective action."

According to the intergovernmental perspective, the EU is (or should be) a union of the governments of member states more than of the European citizens. Based on the assumption that all national governments share the same pro-integrationist spirit, this perspective assigns the intergovernmental institutions (primarily the European Council) the task of composing and balancing state claims through a deliberative process that should satisfy the legitimate expectations of each of them (Wessels 2015). The democratic deficit must be reduced by strengthening the role of national parliaments in European politics, rather than that of the European Parliament (Neyer 2015). It is no coincidence that the euro and migration crises led to a clear shift in the decision-making center of gravity toward the European Council. In situations of crisis, however, the internal functioning of the European Council has not worked as expected by its supporters (Fabbrini 2016a). The contrasting interests of national governmental leaders hardened the deliberative process within the European Council, triggering veto games and incentivizing the postponement of undesired decisions. At the same time, facing the domestic necessity of dealing with urgent problems, the leaders of the main countries ended up in imposing decisions (on policies affecting their electoral fortunes) on the other national governmental leaders, according to a logic of power politics at odds with the presumption of the deliberative logic characterizing the European Council.

From a legitimacy perspective (on legitimacy, an important discussion is Piattoni 2015), both (parliamentary and intergovernmental) statist paradigms display significant limits. For intergovernmentalists, the combination of centralization without democratization, as it takes place within the Eurozone, is not a problem if national leaders and ministers remain accountable to their domestic legislatures. Here, legitimacy is a by-product of the existence of national democracies and not of the functioning of a supranational democracy. For them, the European Council should indeed promote a regular dialogue with national parliaments. This paradigm underestimates, however, that the Brussels-based intergovernmental institutions make decisions in their collegiality, while their members can respond only individually to their legislature. If the intergovernmental bodies make decisions for the whole Eurozone, then they must be legitimated by democratic processes involving the citizens of the whole Eurozone. National leaders are instead legitimated by the citizens of their state, not by the citizens of the Eurozone. For intergovernmentalists, legitimacy is a taxi to take from their own capital to Brussels.

For parliamentarists, the transferring of sovereignty to the Brussels level should be accompanied by the strengthening of the European Parliament, the institution representing European citizens. To be fully legitimized, the EU should adopt the governance model of a parliamentary federal state, i.e., a state functioning on the basis of competition among European-level political parties that seek to win control of the Commission (as the sole European government) through the electoral participation of citizens. Here, legitimacy comes from transnational party competition for electing the members of the European Parliament. This paradigm assumes the EU as mainly a union of citizens rather than of states (or at least it assumes the former to be more important than the latter). Parliamentarists underestimate, however, the implications for parliamentary governance of representing citizens of demographically asymmetric states with different national identities. A union with these systemic features, as the EU is, cannot squeeze its representation patterns into a solely partisan axis (as in parliamentary systems). The EU's legitimacy should come not only from the citizens but also from the states (as political subjects). If the EU is considered a union of states and citizens, then both the parliamentarist and the intergovernmental perspectives are unilateral. The former struggles to legitimize national governments as players in the EU decision-making process; the latter struggles to recognize that democratic legitimacy should come from the citizens represented at the level at which decisions are made. In sum, each of the two positions fails to deal with the complexity of an aggregation of asymmetric and differentiated states. Is an alternative governance's model conceivable?

Beyond the Statist Paradigm: The Federal Union

The reasons for the difficulties met by both the parliamentary and intergovernmental perspectives must be sought in their conceptual premises. For both perspectives, an "ever closer union" means the building of a European polity with statist features. Both perspectives miss the analytical distinction between a nation state and a union of states. It is necessary to resort to the experience of democratic federations for better understanding the logic that presides over the aggregation of states (on the literature of comparative federalism, see Fossum and Jachtenfuchs 2017 and Kelemen and Nicolaidis 2007). That experience shows the existence of a significant distinction between federations emerged from the disaggregation of previously unitary states (federal states) and federations emerged from the aggregation of previously independent states (federal unions) (in this regard, the literature is vast; see the pioneering work by Sbragia 1992 and the widely quoted Stepan 1999). The different origins of the two federal experiences have affected the institutional logic of "coming together" and "holding together" types of federations, complicating the distinction between federation and confederation. Although historians (Hendrickson 2003: xi) considered the federal union "a case of cooperative ventures among states" closer to the confederal rather than federal type, from an empirical perspective the distinction between federation and confederation is too formalistic to be analytically useful, because it omits the case of federations with confederal features (important for conceptualizing the EU experience).

The distinction, within the genus of federations, between federal state and federal union allows us to consider the latter as a federation with confederal features because of its genetic formation. If the federal union is a constitutionalized union of states historically formed through the aggregation of previously independent units with their citizens, then its confederal features are inevitable. Federal unions aggregate states displaying substantial differences in their demography and expressing historically rooted diversity in their national identity. Empirically, in only two cases (the US and Switzerland) has the aggregation ended up forming a successful, constitutionally based federal union (Fabbrini 2010; Kelemen 2014). Their constitutions formalize a pact between the elites of states or cantons to divide sovereignty vertically between levels of government and horizontally between governmental institutions. Horizontally, federal unions institutionalize confederal features through the upper chamber, respectively the US Senate and the Swiss Council of States, where the states are afforded the same power of representation regardless of their population, a confederal feature that, in the case of the US, also affects the state Electoral College for the indirect election of the president. Because it was the states that started the process of aggregation, they could maintain local control over most public policies and could guarantee their confederal representation at the federal center. Vertically, the states are separated from the center through a delimitation of the latter's competences, thus also preventing the possibility that one or a group of them could control the center. At the same time, federal unions are characterized by enumerated powers at the center, whose governmental institutions are in turn separated to prevent the center's domination over the states.

Multiple separation of powers has triggered horizontal political processes without discarding the necessity to regulate them according to criteria of democratic legitimacy. The politicians involved in those policy-making processes represent, and account to, separate constituencies that operate through different temporal mandates; nevertheless, all are entitled to contribute to the decision-making outcomes. The governance structure of a federal union has thus had to solve a puzzle different from that of a federal state, i.e., unitary state or state-like dominion passed through a process of territorial decentralization (as is the case, in Europe, of Germany, Austria, and Belgium, and of highly decentralized countries such as Spain and the United Kingdom; and, outside of Europe, of Australia and to a limited extent Canada, with regard to established democracies). If nation states have historically emerged from a process of cultural homogenization of citizens living within internationally recognized territorial boundaries, the federalization of some of them consisted in decentralizing competences to their territorial units in a context of relative cultural uniformity. All aforementioned federal or quasi-federal states have, in fact, adopted one form or another of fusion of powers or parliamentary government (which centralizes power in the executive or cabinet dependent on the political confidence of the legislature's lower chamber, although mitigated by the sectorial competences of the higher chamber representing the territorial units), whereas the only two successful federal unions have adopted one form or another of separation of powers, although with a monocratic (the US) or collegial (Switzerland) executive (Fabbrini 2017a). It would be implausible to integrate a distinct nation or even the claims to nationhood through some form of horizontal centralization.

Historically, the federal union constitutes the solution to James Madison's paradox of creating a republic of many republics with the 1787 constitutional pact elaborated in Philadelphia. During that convention, Onuf (1983: 197–219) wrote (italics added), "The debasement of state sovereignty was a crucial component in rethinking and reconstituting the American union. But it was also necessary to articulate new images of the union that would resolve *the apparent paradox of sovereign states in a sovereign union*. This was the Federalists' greatest achievement." That achievement was made possible by the empirical division of sovereignty between the federated states and the federal center. The solution of that paradox emerged pragmatically through the mediation between the view of nationalists (including Madison himself) and that of the defenders of states' rights. The idea of divided sovereignty emerged out of political expediency rather than constitutional theory (Ellis 2015; Klarman 2016). It has been argued (Grimm 2015) that the solution eventually found (to pass sovereignty to the people, thus letting them subsequently divide it, through a constitution expressing their will, between the various separate levels of government and the various separate branches constituting each level) is formally coherent with the Westphalian idea of a unitary concept of sovereignty. However, "confronted with the accusation that 'We the People' of the Preamble meant the people of a consolidated nation, Federalists explained that the states could not be enumerated without unreasonably presuming they would join; the phrase meant 'We the People of the

Several States,' each a body politic solely accountable for the act of ratification" (Hendrickson 2003: 13).

Indeed, in setting up a republic of many republics, the US Constitution makers moved beyond Westphalia, transforming sovereignty from a juridical (undivided) to an empirical (divisible) concept. In Philadelphia, sovereignty was divided without cancelling it. It was empirically fragmented in accordance with policy lines so as to guarantee ultimate sovereignty (or decision-making power) in separate policy areas either to the federated states or to the federal center. In those policy areas, one or another is sovereign. It was a genuine paradigmatic revolution, not only because there was a desire to show that democracy would be all the safer the larger and more differentiated the political system that housed it, but above all because they decided to try an unprecedented path, one that interprets sovereignty as a divisible property of public authority. Thus, Madison's analytical framework does not imply a zero-sum redistribution of doses of the same sovereignty between different institutional settings, as in a federal state. Nor does it assume that the complexity of a republic of many republics could be handled only through an internally differentiated confederal polity. Madison's framework envisages that the preferred distribution of policies between the national and supranational levels be negotiated and then enshrined in a constitutional pact, with a limited and enumerated distribution of policies assigned to the federal center and all the rest to the federated states. James Madison writes in *The Federalist* No. 51, "In the compound republic of America, the power surrendered by the people is first divided between two distinct governments, and then the portion allotted to each subdivided among distinct and separate departments. Hence a double security arises to the rights of the people. The different governments will control each other, at the same time that each will be controlled by itself" (now in Beard 1948: 227). The solution of the Federalists' paradox lay in a political decision, of a constitutional status, identifying the dividing line between self-government and shared government (Elazar 1987). That dividing line, in the US and then in Switzerland, means the following: The policies handled by the federal center are limited but with a general jurisdictional value in their application (i.e., they do not allow opt-outs to those who are part of the federation) (Kelemen 2014) and with autonomous (particularly fiscal) resources to manage them (although the acquisition of those resources was highly contrasted by federated states/cantons; Wozniakowski 2017).

The Madisonian approach has an explicit anti-centralizing bias because it fragments sovereignty among distinct institutional entities rather than transferring a chosen amount of general sovereignty from one level (the federated state or canton) to a higher level (the federal center). That political decision identifies and separates the policies to be shared at the federal center's level from those that must remain at the state/canton level. A sovereign union of sovereign states is based on multiple levels of decision-making, not on multiple forms of decision-making within the same level (as in the differentiated governance of the EU). At the same time, democratic legitimacy is promoted by a multiplicity of institutional forms combining state and citizen representation at the various separate levels of the decision-making system. Legitimacy too is separate, as is the accountability of the representatives to the different constituencies that elected them. The politicians elected at the various levels of the union are involved in a permanent negotiation's process on where to fix the competences between one level and the other of government. Parties and party systems play a crucial role in bridging both vertical and horizontal separate institutions, thus making possible their cooperation. Indeed, when they are not able to do that (as in the 1861–1865 US Civil War), the federal union collapses.

Separation of powers means that federal unions have no government as the single institution of the last decision. The government is, rather, a process involving representatives operating within and through different and separate institutions. At the same time, they have no state as an encompassing organization subsuming its territorial units. Sovereignty is divided between federated states and a federal center, preventing the latter from controlling the former. In Europe, conversely (and with exception of Switzerland), the concept of federalism has never been dissociated from the concept of state with its national government. For this reason, federalism has been considered as an organizational variant of the nation state. And it is for this reason that the experience of the EU has struggled to find the necessary concepts with which to define its political development. Let's look more closely at the structure of the US governance as the prototype of multiple separation of powers.

The Governance Structure of a Federal Union: The American Experience

There are more than a few who think that the US is a federal state, not much different from the nation states that have characterized the political history of modern Europe. Nothing could be more wrong. This mistake is made because the US is seen for what it has become in the post-Second World War period, i.e., a global power that acts in international relations as a Westphalian state. The US is not a nation state because of genetic reasons (it aggregated independent states with their own cultural identity, identified by Woodward 2012 as twelve genuine national identities). But it has difficulty in developing as a nation state because of its governance structure. Although neither the noun "federalism" nor the adjective "federal" appears in its constitutional documents, the US is a federal union based on the intertwining of federal and confederal aspects (Dahl 2006). The US adopted an institutional system that combined interstate with suprastate arrangements, without establishing ex ante which side (interstate or suprastate) must be considered as preeminent. And this combination has been the target of reasoned criticisms (Dahl 2003).

Institutionally, the US has been organized around a separation of powers that is both vertical (between the federated states and the federal center) and horizontal (between the institutions of the federal center). This has made it, and makes it, different from a federal state. The federal state requires the former separation but not the latter. In vertical terms, the federal state can claim to represent the interests of the nation or of the federation as no federated unit could do. Federal states are separated in terms of vertical (territorial) relations but are fused in terms of horizontal (governmental) relations. The US represents the first attempt at building instead a political system based on a double separation. The horizontal separation has taken the form of the formula that the government consists of separate institutions sharing power (Neustadt 1990). In other words, this formula is set up with the following terms: a president (executive power), elected indirectly through the Electoral College who can serve for four years (and renewable only once, since the Twenty-Second Amendment of the Constitution of 1951); a House of Representatives elected directly in districts within the individual states, with representatives who serve for two years; a Senate consisting of two senators for each state, who serve for six years (one-third of which coincides with the biennial election of the House of Representatives). Until the Seventeenth Amendment of 1913, the senators were appointed by legislatures of the respective states. After that year, they were elected directly by the electors in constituencies equivalent to the size of each individual state. Finally, the Supreme Court (consisting of nine judges appointed by the president, with, as the Constitution states, the "advice and consent" of the Senate, who can serve for life) is responsible for resolving disputes between not only the separate institutions but also the latter and the citizens over the reach of public power. Where is the government, in the sense of the decision-making institution of last resort, in this system of separation of powers?

The US system has been defined as a hybrid (Fukuyama 2014: part IV). It maintains the confederal principles (such as the representation of two senators per state, regardless of the population of the state, or Electoral College of the states for the election of the president consisting of grand electors of an equivalent number to the members of the House of Representatives and to the senators of the state, thus over-representing the smaller states through the Senate), albeit introducing more directly federal principles (such as the allocation to the center of exclusive competence in the field of military security and foreign or justice policy). Also, where the federal center has exclusive competence, the exercise of its federal authority is subject to specific limitations. Not only are the federal institutions separated, but the functioning of a separate institution requires the collaboration of other separate institutions. This is the principle of checks and balances that was introduced in Philadelphia to make it possible for a system of separate government to function. For example, the "advice and consent" of the Senate is necessary for the approval (with a qualified majority vote of two-thirds of the members) of international treaties signed by the president, or to make presidential appointments of members of the executive or judges of the Supreme Court operative. Indeed, on the crucial issues of foreign and justice policy, the chamber of the states (the Senate) has maintained for itself the role of main controller of the executive.

Despite the disagreements at the Convention of Philadelphia, the federal center was initially attributed two crucial responsibilities: promoting economic growth (internally) and managing war and peace (externally). Let us look at the first responsibility. The Commerce Clause of the Constitution (Art. 1, VIII.3) allocated to the federal

Congress the power to eliminate state barriers to trade, both within the federation and between the latter and other countries. Through this clause it was possible to create a free trade area among the member states of the federation, which was then extended to the various states and territories that became members of the federation through the various enlargements. At the same time, the Contracts Clause of the Constitution (Art. 1, X.1) removed from the states the power to approve legislation that could call into question respect of contracts signed between private contracting parties, thus guaranteeing the juridical bases of the market. Finally, the Constitution (Art. 1, X.1) created a monetary union, giving the federal center the exclusive power to coin the common currency, and then a budget union, giving the Congress the power of indirect taxation and subsequently also direct taxation (with the Sixteenth Amendment of the Constitution of 1913). Regarding the second responsibility, the Constitution prohibited individual member states from creating military alliances between themselves, or from joining alliances with other countries, or from pursuing their own foreign policy. The federal center has the exclusive power over war and peace, even if this power must be exercised within rigid constitutional limitations (on the basis of which wars are *declared* by the Congress, as per Art. 1, VIII.11, and *made* by the president as commander in chief of the armed forces, as per Art. 2, II.1) (Crabb and Holt 1992; Fisher 2013). At the same time, the federated states were recognized as having the power (which they already had before creating the union) of equipping themselves with their own defense (militia), so that the military force of the union continues to have a compound nature (combining the force of the states and that acquired by the center). With the creation of a modern military establishment after the Second World War (and the related formation of a Defense Department within the presidency), defense has been centralized by the federal center, without, however, weakening state militias.

The separation of powers also functions vertically. US federalism was created and institutionalized as a dual federalism (Elazar 1987). The federal center and the federated states have been equipped with the same institutional structure of government (based on the separation of powers) and have been organized to carry out the same legislative, executive, and judicial functions, but are bound to affirm their sovereignty in distinct policy areas. A federal state, as an entity above the federated states, was prevented from emerging in order not to threaten the specific sovereignty of the latter. The strengthening of the federal center (starting from the end of the nineteenth century; Skowroneck 1982) has not meant the weakening of the powers of the federated states. Dual federalism has inevitably been shaken by the transformations that have occurred over the two-century-long history of the country. After the 1861–1865 Civil War, the process of nationalization increased significantly, also thanks to constitutional amendments thirteen (1865), fourteen (1868), and fifteen (1870). After those amendments, the constitutional doctrine was affirmed that the federated states, and not only the federal center, were required to respect the Bill of Rights consisting of the first ten amendments to the Constitution (1791). As an effect of the nationalization of the country, at the end of the nineteenth century the habit spread of talking (in specialist terms as well as in everyday language) of the United States in the singular and no longer in the plural ("the United States is" instead of "the United States are"; Sbragia 1992). Following that, it was the industrial transformations (at the end of nineteenth century) and the growing international role of the US (after the First World War and, above all, the Second World War) that led to an extension of the prerogatives of the federal center (Hendrickson 2009; Katznelson and Shefter 2002) through an increase in the number of policies controlled by the latter.

The constitutional constraints on centralization, however, have continued to operate. According to Hoffman, Parsons, and Springer (2017) and Egan (2015), for instance, the US single market is still much less integrated than the EU single market, because of the US states' capacity to preserve their own powers and competences vis-à-vis the federal center. The Constitution has continued to guarantee the sovereignty of the states in specific policy fields. In turn, the decisions of the Supreme Court have periodically alternated the defense of the rights of the states and the promotion of the needs of the federal center. Thus, after the strong movement in favor of federal centralization that was seen between the 1920s and the 1970s, starting from the 1980s there was a countermovement in favor of policy decentralization to the federated states. But because the federal center has continued to control important resources for policies of interest to the states, consequently dual federalism has gradually transformed into federalism with cooperative practices (Schutze 2010). The federal center, for example, uses grants-in-aid programs for making financial resources available to the states provided their acceptance of the objectives and criteria set up

by it. Although vertical separation of powers has functioned like
a pendulum (Beer 1993), alternating periods of centralization and
decentralization, the tendency has been toward an increase of the
resources and role of the federal center (owing to structural factors,
such as the increasing complexity of domestic policies and the global
role played by the country). The outcome has been a policy state that
"finds itself, and the polity it governs, unhinged, unmoored, adrift"
(Orren and Skowroneck 2017: 8) or, better, an "unsustainable
American state" (Jacobs and King 2009).

In the US governance structure, the logic of the functioning of the
vertical separation of powers has constantly intertwined with the functional logic of the horizontal separation of powers. In the nineteenth
century, the federal system also kept a decentralized structure because
the power of the federal center rotated around the Congress (it was
called a system of congressional government). The nationalization and
internationalization of the subsequent century led to the formation of
a federal center apparatus that supported the growth of the president's
role and the construction of the modern presidency (it is called a system
of presidential government). Although the power of the states is still
constitutionally intact, the global role played by the US constitutes
a formidable incentive to strengthen the federal center and the president vis-à-vis the federated states. The US continues to be (internally)
a federal union, but its international role forces the country to act
(externally) as a Westphalian state. Despite the presidentialization of
the federal center, the US cannot be assimilated into a nation state,
owing to the constitutional impossibility of resolving interinstitutional
conflicts through horizontal and vertical centralization of decision-
making (Polsby 2008). Indeed, the federal center continues to be contested when it claims an authority superior to those of the federated
states. Once it is acknowledged that the governance's logic of a federal
union is based on multiple separation of powers (considering the US as
the paradigmatic case), then it is possible to investigate how that logic
can be analytically applied to the EU.

The Governance Structure of a European Federal Union

A federal union respecting democratic criteria must prevent any confusion of powers between the executive and legislative functions in the
policy realms entrusted to the institutions operating at the center and

between the latter and the national level of government. Regarding vertical governance, it is necessary to prevent confusion of powers between domestic and supranational institutions. That means the obstruction of the road allowing national governmental leaders to come to exercise supranational governmental power. The supranational role of national governments should be acknowledged but reframed. National governments can play a direct role in the supranational legislature but not a direct role in the supranational executive (in the US, the governors of the federated states have no voice in the functioning of the federal executive). At the same time, national parliaments should deal with national issues and not intrude in supranational issues (that should be the province of the European Parliament). The subsidiarity clause is not sufficient for guaranteeing a firewall between national and supranational levels of government, if it is not strengthened by an institutional separation between the latter.

Regarding horizontal governance, the analytical exercise is necessarily more complex. To make the governance of a federal union legitimate and effective, it requires, first, the institutionalization of a single decision-making regime for the policies to manage at the supranational level and, second, the institutionalization of a separation between the executive and legislative branches. In relation to executive power, it is necessary to acknowledge that the executive emerged in the EU is the result of a double systemic need to express, with the president of the Commission, the preferences of the European citizens through the European Parliament and, with the president of the European Council, those of the member states through their governments. If the European Council is the elephant in the executive power's room, how should it be handled? Certainly, the problem could be solved by taking the elephant out of the room. If the presidencies of the European Council and of the Commission are merged into the latter, as something that is not prohibited by the Lisbon Treaty, there would be a return to a unified presidency required to respond primarily to the European Parliament. As proposed by the Commission's president, Juncker, in his September 13, 2017, State of the Union Address, "Europe would function better if we were to merge the Presidents of the European Council and the European Commission. (...) Europe would be easier to understand if one captain was steering the ship. Having a single President would simply better reflect the true nature of our European Union as both a Union of States and a Union of citizens."

However, a single president (if accountable to the European Parliament) would have difficulty in balancing states and citizens. In fact, although the chamber representing the national ministers (the Council of Ministers) would continue to play its intergovernmental role, nevertheless the European Parliament would become the real political center of the EU. Heads of governments representing states with powerful national identities and consolidated configurations of power would find it hard to accept to being dominated by the European Parliament that would have the power to elect the single president. This is the case in Germany where the chancellor is accountable to the *Bundestag* and in Canada where the prime minister is accountable to the House of Commons, thus reducing national governmental leaders to the status of minister-presidents or prime ministers of a German *Land* or a Canadian province. If the elephant of national governments should leave the room of executive power, at the same time the latter cannot fall under the control of the European Parliament as representative of the European citizens, as it sought to do with the strategy of the *Spitzenkandidaten* in relation to the election of the president of the Commission. The EU executive power's puzzle can be solved only by recognizing both of its sides through a strategy of separation of powers that promotes an independent dual executive (constituted by a president of the Union, rather than of the European Council, and the president of the Commission) operating under the powers of checks and balances of the bicameral legislature (separately representing member states and European citizens).

In this dual executive, the member state side cannot be represented by the president of the European Council as it is currently defined by the Lisbon Treaty. If it is agreed that it is systemically necessary to introduce a firewall between national governments and EU executive officers, then it would be implausible to have a president elected by (a qualified majority of the members of) the European Council (and dependent on them, so much so that the current president does not have even voting power in that body). It would be also implausible to have, in a federal union of asymmetric and differentiated states, a direct election of an executive officer. Any direct election would lead to the permanent hegemony of the most populous states (exactly as the parliamentary election of a single president would favor the representatives of the larger states at the detriment of the smaller states). The strategy to be followed could instead be that of the Electoral College, with the European Council having the role of initiating the electoral process but not concluding it. In this framework, the members of the European Council select two candidates for the role of president of the Union (through an electoral procedure established autonomously by them). The two candidates are then subject to the vote of presidential electors organized in national electoral colleges. Each electoral college consists of a number of presidential electors who are equivalent to the number of seats in the European Parliament held by that country. The means of electing the presidential electors must be established by the individual member states (although their popular election would increase the legitimacy of the process). Because the distribution of the seats in the European Parliament takes into account the population of each individual member state, but with an over-representation of small and medium-size member states (owing to the criterion of *degressive proportionality*), the asymmetrical nature of the EU is (in some way) taken into consideration, but above all the separation of powers between the executive and legislature is institutionalized (for the very reason that the European Parliament and its members have no role in the electoral process). The two candidates will undertake their electoral campaign by putting forward their program in the member states. Because there is no quorum set for votes to legitimate the election, the person elected as president of the Union will be the candidate, between the two candidates put forward, obtaining the absolute majority of votes of the presidential electors of the various national electoral colleges (thus guaranteeing their political legitimacy). An electoral process based on the competition between only two candidates will inevitably guarantee a majority's outcome. In a large union of states, a run-off election might be too cumbersome and costly. The electoral colleges will be immediately dissolved after the election of the president, because the president must account to the bicameral legislature and not to those who elected her. The European Council would thus turn into the highest formation of the Council, gathering when crucial legislative measures are submitted by the executive of the EU. Or it might be transformed into a seniors' advisory board of the president-elect, without, however, any decision-making power to exercise on the latter's choices.

Although the procedure to nominate the president of the European Commission may remain the same, i.e., ending with the vote of the European Parliament, it should be formalized that that vote does not express a relation of political confidence between the two institutions.

Rather, the parliamentary vote must have the characteristics of "advise and consent" as happens in separation of powers systems (approving the Commission's president and the individual commissioners, not the Commission as a whole). An institutional trade-off would take place. The repeal of the European Council's executive role is offset by the exclusion of any political confidence relation between the European Parliament and the Commission. The two heads of the executive will therefore have distinct legitimizations. The legitimization of the president of the Union will derive first from the national governmental leaders (who decide the short list of the two candidates in competition) and then from the national electoral colleges (which choose from the short list), while the legitimization of the president of the Commission will derive from the European Parliament (or, better, from the elections of the latter). At the same time, the legitimization of the commissioners who make up the operational structure of the dual executive must combine the wishes of national governments with the preferences of the bicameral legislature as mediated by the two presidents. Which of the two heads of the dual executive will be predominant will then depend on the policies as well as on their respective personalities, although it will be the president of the Union who will represent the organization both internally and externally. At the same time, it is necessary to strengthen the operational link between the president of the Union and the president of the Commission, formalizing the system of the dual executive. It would fall to the Commission, and not to the General Secretariat of the Council of Ministers, to prepare the deliberations of the dual executive and submit the latter's decisions to the legislature (where the Council of Ministers or the European Council will be supported by the General Secretariat). Citizens will thus have the possibility, with the, albeit indirect, election of the president of the Union to influence the choices of the supranational executive, exactly as they can influence those choices by taking part in the elections for the European Parliament from which the support for the president of the Commission will derive. Indeed, the two elections (the indirect one of the president of the Union and the direct one of the European Parliament) might be coterminous, with the former briefly preceding the latter for riding the coattails of its outcome.

Once the executive and its dual composition have been formalized, it will then fall to the Council of Ministers (plus the European Council) and the European Parliament to exercise control over the proposals and the choices that it will put forward, control that will be all the more effective the more the two legislative chambers are not bound by a relation of political confidence with the dual executive. An effective executive requires adequate checks and balances by the legislature. Moreover, the bicameral legislature should be equipped with the power to put forward laws and an autonomous (although limited) budget (derived from an independent taxing power) for supporting the center's policies. The EU has indeed come to be characterized as having adopted (with the 1979 direct election of the European Parliament) the principle of representation without taxation, which is as undemocratic as its opposite (i.e., taxation without representation, from which started the US struggle for liberation against English colonialism symbolized by the Declaration of Independence of 1776) (Fabbrini 2016d). The bicameral legislature of a federal union should have available an autonomous budget, limited but not bound by previous agreements between the states, deriving from taxation that is independent from national transfers. This budget should be one with which to realize, for instance, the union's anti-cyclical policies (such as, in crisis conditions, a program targeting youth unemployment or to support investments for European infrastructure), as well as to promote social policies to integrate those of the individual states. A contemporary federal union, in fact, must also be a social union, contrary to the federal union created in Philadelphia at the end of the eighteenth century or in Berne in the mid-nineteenth century. The complexity of the social problems is such that it cannot be addressed only with the public policy instruments that states hold (Ferrera 2017). Without autonomous and specific resources and competences (although necessarily limited), the direct election of the European Parliament or the indirect election of the Council of Ministers would have no political meaning. The strength (supported by resources and prerogatives) of legislative power is a necessary condition to guarantee the democratic nature of the federal union. An autonomous budget is the pre-condition for democratizing the governance system (Barbieri and Vallée 2017). The politicization of the president of the Union's election would allow the Commission to maintain its technical and administrative character. The dual executive could thus help combine politics with the technical side, electoral consensus with policy competences. Even the complex multilevel system of a union of states can meet the requirements of the division of powers in the form of separation of institutions and sharing of functions.

Conclusion

The debate on the EU governance should be enriched by a better understanding of the federations' experience. When the limits of the intergovernmental governance are acknowledged, the alternative proposed cannot be the parliamentary governance, that is, to bring the strategic policies of the intergovernmental constitution within the institutional logic of the supranational constitution twisted in a parliamentary direction. This is unrealistic, not only because the supranational method expresses a form of parliamentarism that has a statist connotation, but also because the European Parliament's preeminence would be refused by national governments that have shown their influence and determination in guaranteeing themselves a decision-making role. The response to the question requires abandoning the unsatisfactory dichotomy between the perspective of parliamentary union and the perspective of intergovernmental union. Both perspectives reflect a statist vision of the integration process, with its corollary of decision-making centralization and vertical overlapping (if not fusion; see Wessels 1997) of the levels of government. If we move away from the statist model and go toward the construction of a federal union, then the alternative to centralization will be easier to identify. The demographic differences between member states cannot be regulated by mechanisms of parliamentary or intergovernmental centralization. At the same time, their national identity's differences cannot be considered contingent factors that are destined to be overcome by the integration process. It is necessary to settle them without denying them. A new governance model is needed, that of the union of states and citizens that functions in accordance with one version or another of the logic of the multiple separation of powers. A democratic union of states and citizens presupposes, for functioning, the acknowledgment of its compound nature, protected by reciprocally separate institutions, vertically and horizontally.

Unions of asymmetrical states, whose citizenships have different national identities, are necessarily contradictory projects. They institutionalize an inevitable tension between the logic of the union of citizens and that of the union of states. From a comparative perspective, they are federal unions because they combine the aspects of a federation with those of a confederation. Federal unions cannot be reconciled with suprastate or supranational centralization (even if electorally legitimated). If this logic is accepted, then neither the EU nor the Eurozone has found a solution to the clash between the interests of the states (and of their governments) and those of the citizens. A federal union must overcome the contrast between the two constitutions, identifying an institutional architecture for all the policies assigned, an original version of the strategy of the multiple separation of powers. A federal union must prevent any confusion of powers between the executive and legislative functions as well as overlapping of competences and institutions between levels of government. The (multiple) separation of powers is an institutional strategy (Brinkley, Polsby, and Sullivan 1997), not a defined model. What counts is its ability to generate decisions without turning (at the horizontal level) to hierarchical centralization or institutionalized hegemony and (at the vertical level) to the reciprocal direct influence between levels of government. It will then fall to the European Court of Justice to guarantee respect of the founding principles of the political pact that has formalized the union, as well as to resolve the disputes between the states that have signed that pact or between the institutions that make it work. Will the federal union's paradigm be inspiring for conceptualizing the future of Europe?

5 | The Future of Europe as Constitutional Decoupling

Introduction

This book has argued that the crisis of the EU has ended up being of an institutional nature. The compromises between different visions on the purpose of integration have been altered or called into question by the multiple crises of the 2010s and their magnitude. Under the pressure of events, in the context of the institutional structure of the Lisbon Treaty, national governments deepened their control of the decision-making process in the strategic policies affected by those crises, seeking solutions thus challenged or contrasted owing to their different views or interests. These differences have fed a reciprocal lack of trust between national governments, which, in turn, has driven toward further administrative and legal centralization with the aim of de-politicizing the decision-making process. Even when national governments positively managed those crises, they pressed on with ad hoc solutions for ad hoc problems, with no vision on how to connect one solution to the other. Probably it was thought that this is the way the integration process advances. Indeed, there is a widespread opinion, in Brussels and national capitals, that the experience of European integration is made up of contingent solutions in order to respond to contingent problems, a sort of integration by necessity. After all, the thinking goes, the EU is something special, so don't dare compare it with other experiences of aggregation of states. As Genschel and Jachtenfuchs (2016: 185) argued, "In the short term, this buys time and might help to alleviate the immediate symptoms of the crisis, to conceal the huge redistributive implication of the crisis and thus to keep constraining dissensus at bay. In a medium- to long-term perspective, however, this does not improve input legitimacy but rather risks to decrease it and to increase constraining dissensus."

112

Scholars (Weiler 1999) have developed an argument on the EU as a sui generis system, an organization assumed to have no historic precedents. In turn, the idea of European exceptionalism has exonerated the taking into consideration the basic principles of organizing a democratic union of states, such as those of the division of powers and the balancing between institutions organizing its decision-making process. The ideology of sui generis, when faced with unexpectedly serious challenges, has led to processes of institutionalizing the EU based on the confusion of powers, on the multiplication of legal orders, and on the formalization of intergovernmental arrangements bereft of any democratic legitimacy. The multiple crises of the 2010s, the 2016 Brexit and neo-nationalist US presidency, and the growth of populism and nationalism have triggered a debate on the future of the EU and the reform of the Eurozone. New formulas have been elaborated or old ones reinterpreted, in a pinwheel of words never clearly conceptualized. Concepts (such as *Europe à la carte, multispeed Europe, concentric circles Europe*) have been used as equivalent terms, although they are reciprocally distinctive. It is necessary to clarify this debate for better identifying the various theoretical alternatives. The chapter is organized as follows: First, it synthetizes the official debate on the future of Europe for showing its indifference to the governance's issues. Second, it conceptualizes the main governance's paradigms that a union of states should theoretically consider. Third, it identifies (through a comparative analysis) the political logic constituting a democratic union of states. Fourth, it develops the argument for moving from policy differentiation to constitutional decoupling of the EU.

The Future of Europe's Debate

The debate on the future of Europe has become a growth industry. Here I will consider the main official documents elaborated by the EU institutions or by national crucial actors (as central bank governors), leaving aside the vast literature generated by private organizations, think tanks, and single national governments. The debate was inaugurated by the Four Presidents' Report of June 2012 on "Towards a Genuine Economic and Monetary Union" (Van Rompuy 2012), which was followed by the Five Presidents' report of June 2015 on "Completing Europe's Economic and Monetary Union" (Juncker et al.

2015). Interestingly, both reports go into detail with specific policy regimes (economic union, financial union, fiscal union) to be implemented, but remain vague on the democratic legitimacy of the Eurozone governance (which gives the title to their last, brief chapter). In a document subsequent to that of the Five Presidents, the Commission (European Commission 2015) took it upon itself to translate into operational terms the concept of a new economic governance (proposed by the reports of the Four and Five Presidents). The core of the new governance's proposal of the Commission was represented by the transformation of the president of the Eurogroup into the finance minister of the Eurozone, with the task of representing the latter in international financial bodies, starting with the International Monetary Fund. This minister should be chosen, as currently happens, by the other finance ministers of the Eurozone and should operate in collaboration with an independent European fiscal council. The finance minister of the Eurozone should have preeminent authority over the national budgets, using a specific Eurozone budget to support national adjustment policies. Of course, the European Parliament must be informed (informed, note) of the choices that are made as needed. But it has no power of approval or sanction. Surprisingly, the Commission ended up in proposing the strengthening of intergovernmental centralization rather than calling it into question.

Central bankers too intervened in this debate, in the form of an article (titled "Europe at the Crossroads") jointly signed by the governors of the *Banque de France* and of the *Bundesbank* and published in both *Le Monde* and *Süddeutschen Zeitung* on February 8, 2016. It is a remarkable contribution because it considers the political implications of policy reform. The two central bank governors wrote that "euro-area member states would have to allow a comprehensive sharing of sovereignty and powers at the European level, which, in turn, would require greater democratic accountability. (...) It is up to politicians to design the new framework, but they could build on, for example, the following factors: an efficient and less fragmented European administration; a common Treasury for the euro area in conjunction with an independent fiscal council; and a stronger political body for policy decisions under parliamentary control. (...) However, if governments and parliaments in the euro area were to shy away from the political dimension of a fully-fledged union, this would leave just one viable option – a decentralised approach based on individual responsibility and even stronger rules. Under this scheme, the fiscal rules, which have already been reinforced through the fiscal compact and the European semester particularly, would have to be strengthened. In such a regime of increased individual responsibility, we would also have to make sure that risk, including that of sovereign exposures, is properly taken into account by all stakeholders – not least to reduce the vulnerability of banks should sovereigns run into financial troubles. (...) Taking this direction would retain national sovereignty within the euro area – with a correspondingly lower level of solidarity."

The two central bank governors' proposal has the advantage of stating a clear alternative. Either the Eurozone moves toward further centralization of the economic and fiscal policy of its member states or economic and fiscal policy must be left to the control of the member states, but within an even more intrusive regulatory system and without mechanisms of reciprocal solidarity between member states. In budget policies, either the move is toward a transfer of sovereignty from the member states to the intergovernmental institutions of Brussels, or toward a further decentralization of those policies that, however, should be under even stricter rules for neutralizing the possibility of moral hazard. Decentralization is still incompatible with any policy of solidarity between member states. If countries want to preserve their sovereignty over the budget, then they will have to deal with crises by themselves. Of course, the preference of the two central bank governors is for the first option, which is considered to be the only one that can preserve the Eurozone. After all, national central bankers, and above all the European Central Bank in Frankfurt, have long been asking to have a political interlocutor in Brussels. The Eurozone (for them) cannot survive using only monetary policy. For the European Central Bank, it is necessary that a government be formed for economic policy, i.e., an institution allowed to pursue a coordinated economic policy derived from the nineteen national economic policies (of the member states of the Eurozone) – an institution politically balancing the monetary policy pursued by the European Central Bank. The preoccupation of the European Central Bank is most likely the result of a rational calculation: It does not want to shoulder political responsibility because that would confuse its technical neutrality (Henning 2016). Thus, for the central bank governors, the government of a union of states necessarily implies the centralization of the decision-making process, let alone its judicialization.

What emerges from these documents is a perspective of centralized economic governance through the institutionalization of a Eurozone finance minister, supported by an independent (from the Commission) European fiscal council, responsible for the Eurozone budget (based on national financial transfers) and required to provide a purely informative report to the European Parliament. In this perspective, the Commission is de facto exonerated from the role of implementing the decisions of the ECOFIN Council. It is the intergovernmental response to the politicization of the Commission – politicization due to the choice by the main European parties to present their *Spitzenkandidat* for the European Parliament elections in May 2014. Thus, because the Commission tried to interpret its post-2014 mandate in political terms (allowing a flexible interpretation of the Stability and Growth Pact by those member states facing "extraordinary challenges"), national governments (with the apparent leadership of Wolfgang Schauble, German minister of finance in the period 2009–2017) were offered the perspective of entrusting control over national budget policies to independent bodies (such as the European fiscal council) and to a finance minister who depends on their decisions as well as on their budgets. If this perspective is not accepted by the debtor countries, then the only alternative will be the return to national sovereignty over the budget, albeit highly regulated, without, however, any mechanisms to protect against future asymmetric shocks, i.e., without interstate solidarity mechanisms. Many wondered why the Commission, with its 2015 Report, accepted that political logic.

The Commission made a further step in this debate through the "White Paper on the Future of Europe," which its president Jean-Claude Juncker presented to the European Parliament on March 1, 2017. The white paper enlarged the perspective through the identification of five scenarios for the post-crisis EU, although in all of them the issue of the governance's model is not specified. The first scenario envisaged is that of "carrying on" the current differentiated system through a policy of "muddling-through" to adapt to the crises. The second scenario, that of "nothing but the single market," goes to pre-Maastricht, advancing the hypothesis of a generalized step back to the 1986 Single European Act. The third scenario is that of letting "those who want more, do more," giving rise to coalitions of those willing to pursue specific programs through forms of enhanced and structured cooperation. The fourth scenario is "doing less more efficiently," and the fifth scenario is that of "doing much more together." The five scenarios offered different options for dealing with the crisis of the EU and the divisions within it. The first option expresses the view of those who argue that it is necessary to make the best of the current differentiation of the EU, rationalizing or fine-tuning it but without opposing its logic. The second option expresses the view of those aiming to conciliate national sovereignty with economic cooperation. The third option expresses the view of those aiming to escape the continuous deadlock in the decision-making process, according to a view traditionally called a "multispeed Europe" (Piris 2012), a view thus celebrated by the Rome Declaration signed on March 25, 2017, by all twenty-seven member states on the occasion of the sixtieth anniversary of the Treaties of Rome. The Declaration stated: "We will act together, at different paces and intensity where necessary, while moving in the same direction, as we have done in the past, in line with the Treaties and keeping the door open to those who want to join later." A few days earlier, at the end of the meeting of the leaders of the four largest post-Brexit member states (Germany, France, Italy, and Spain) held in Versailles on March 6, 2017, the German chancellor declared that "a multispeed Europe is necessary; otherwise we are blocked," thus adding that "we must have the courage to accept that some countries can move forward a little more quickly than others." This third option assumes differentiation as a means (not an end, as in the first option) for neutralizing the veto power of those member states opposing steps forward in the integration's process. The fourth option expresses the view of those aiming to deregulate the EU, making its functioning simpler through focusing on only those policies objectively crucial for the existence of the organization. The fifth option expresses the view of those who argue that internal divisions should be overcome through the formation of a state-like organization. The identification of the five options, although certainly useful for soliciting the debate, might, however, generate misleading if not downright wrong evaluations. Indeed, some of those options easily overlap instead of being clear alternatives. None of them, finally, deals with the form of the governance's model the EU might adopt for meeting the criteria of democratic legitimacy in its functioning.

Alternative Paradigms of Governance

For the foregoing reasons, I propose to conceptualize the future of Europe through three basic governance paradigms, each one accommodating one or more of the policy scenarios identified by the European Commission. The first paradigm consists of the rationalization of the EU as a highly differentiated organization. According to this paradigm, what matters is getting the EU machine to work, generating some public goods where possible, adapting the integration process to the needs (or electoral schedules) of one or another country, but without expecting the EU to function according to democratic principles. James Buchanan's theory of organizations, operating under conditions of internal complexity and external divergent pressures (Buchanan 1965), can offer a theory for conceptualizing a differentiated EU. As Giandomenico Majone (2014) observed, because integration has gone too far, the EU has reached such a level of complexity as to become ungovernable as a unitary organization. In this context, differentiation instead allows the EU to answer specific requests through a variable combination of states interested in participating in specific policies for satisfying those requests. Buchanan's theory of a club of clubs might offer a scientific basis for managing the necessarily expanding internal differentiation of the EU. As Majone argues (2014: 17), the "economic theory of clubs may be used to provide a robust conceptual basis for the analysis of integration à la carte and of other forms of functional integration." From a governance perspective, the EU à la carte would consist of transient combinations of clusters of states dealing with specific problems, whose governments will coordinate within and through the European Council (here interpreted as a sort of diplomatic forum). An internally differentiated European Council will be the center of the *club governance* model. Although technically supported by the Commission, the national leaders will be fully autonomous in their reciprocal negotiation, with the European Court of Justice intervening only to resolve potentially destructive disputes between them. In the club governance model, the European Parliament would be the main institutional loser, while the European Council would be the exclusive institutional winner. The economic theory of clubs is uninterested in the question of the democratic legitimacy of the EU's governance, but it is interested only in the delivering of specific and differentiated policy outcomes. In a Europe à la carte, legitimacy comes indirectly from the results of the decisions made. It is a species of differentiated output legitimacy, to use Scharpf's terminology (2009). For Majone, a club of clubs will be judged mainly by the quality of the services provided rather than by the democratic nature of its governance regime. However, it would be highly questionable for the EU to accommodate its internal differentiation to the point of disregarding the need for its democratic legitimacy.

The club governance paradigm might accommodate the first and third scenarios delineated by the Commission's white paper. It can allow the new treaties (particularly the Fiscal Compact) to be brought back within the juridical system of the EU (as is formally possible as of January 1, 2018). After all, the Fiscal Compact achieved its main objective (through the introduction in the constitution of signatory states of the clause on balanced budget), so it could be incorporated into the Lisbon Treaty as it was made with the Schengen agreement. The integration process would continue to have its unitary nature, regulated by a single legal framework, with internal functional differentiations in relation to specific policies (the most accurate discussion on differentiation in EU law is De Witte, Ott, and Vos 2017; from a political science perspective, see Fossum 2015 and Leuffen, Rittberger, and Schimmelfennig 2013). This paradigm leaves many questions unanswered. It does not deal with the divisions between the member states, particularly with the asymmetric effects of intergovernmentalism. It is hard to imagine, for instance, that the strengthening of the intergovernmental logic (which would take place with the inclusion of the Fiscal Compact in the Lisbon Treaty) and the ordo-liberal philosophy (which the Fiscal Compact celebrates) can keep the Eurozone united. This paradigm does not conceptualize the contrast between the two EU decision-making regimes or constitutions and the institutional uncertainty the contrast produces. At the same time, this strategy increases the degree of confusion in the functioning of the EU. Different policy regimes, structured around differing interinstitutional relations, involving different countries, and loosely coordinated through the European Council, would make it impossible for the citizens to understand what is happening and who makes decisions on the basis of which electoral mandate. A confused, opaque, and ineffective organization is destined to increase citizens' unease with it, forcing them to look for exclusively national solutions to their problems. Theoretically, a club governance model is not compatible with a supranational organization. Indeed, it would expedite the transformation (or involution) of an intergovernmental EU into an international organization.

The second paradigm would aim at overcoming the EU internal differentiation through the institutionalization of a centralized and politically homogeneous organization, with features resembling a state-like polity. It is congenial with the fifth scenario of the Commission's white paper, when it stressed the necessity that "cooperation between all Member States goes further than ever before *in all domains*" (italics added). Each of the twenty-seven member states should relinquish an increasing share of their sovereignty and democracy, transferring it to the institutions in Brussels (the center). Rodrik (2011: ch. 10) was probably the first scholar who conceptualized the trilemma, offering a theoretical basis to this paradigm. According to him, "Democracy, national sovereignty and global economic integration are mutually incompatible: we can combine any two of the three, but never have all three simultaneously and in full" (Rodrik 2007). A higher level of one of them requires a lower level of the others, as in a zero-sum game. Deeper European integration implies less national sovereignty and weaker democratic control at the national level. This state governance paradigm, too, leaves many questions unanswered. It underestimates the differing power of the states involved in the process of integration. The management of the euro crisis, for instance, increased rather than reduced the national sovereignty and power of domestic democratic institutions in the creditor states (in Germany, the *Bundestag* and the Federal Constitutional Court, or *Bundesverfassungsgericht*) (Matthijs 2017), while the opposite happened in the debtor member states (in Greece as well as in Italy, as shown by the outcomes of the March 4, 2018, elections). Moreover, the crisis led to a process of decision-making centralization in the European Council and the ECOFIN Council that created hierarchical relations between creditor and debtor member states. The solution of Rodrik's trilemma would conceptually imply the decision-making centralization as in state organizations, blurring the distinction between national and European levels of government (as envisaged by both parliamentary and intergovernmental perspectives on the political union). State governance implies a highly structured political center, either around the European Council or the European Parliament. The paradigm of state governance might give substance to the formula of *concentric circles Europe*, originally proposed by Wolfgang Schauble and Karl Lamers in their 1994 document "Reflections on European Politics," constituted by a closed group of economically and culturally homogeneous countries (*Kernel Europe*), and by adjacent circles of less integrated states.

It should be observed that the two paradigms can accommodate the processual logic of multispeed Europe (the third scenario of the Commission's white paper). In fact, the processual approach leaves unanswered the question of the governance model that a multispeed Europe might or should take. Indeed, a multispeed Europe might go in opposite directions. It may end up by speeding up the differentiation of the EU, as desired by the club governance's supporters of *Europe à la carte*, or it may increase the centralization of policy making in the most integrated areas (such as the Eurozone), as envisaged by the state governance's supporters of *concentric circles Europe*, or it could go both ways at the same time (high differentiation of the EU plus closer centralization of Eurozone). If multispeed Europe leaves undefined the form of the EU's future governance, and because the other two options are unsatisfactory, then an alternative model of governance, dealing with the challenges of democratic legitimacy in a union of states, should be investigated. Between the paradigm of *club governance* and *state governance*, the paradigm of the *federal union* might be conceptualized.

We need Madison more than Rodrik or Majone to conceptualize the dilemmas of the governance of a union of asymmetrical and differentiated states. The EU is facing Madison's theoretical paradox, that of delineating an original answer to the question of how to reconcile "sovereign states in a sovereign union" (Onuf 1983: 198). Madison solved that paradox pursuing a strategy of constitutional differentiation. That strategy expects that the preferred distribution of policies between the national and supranational levels be negotiated and then enshrined in a constitutional pact. Thus, the solution of the paradox lies in a constitutional decision identifying the dividing line between self-government and shared government (to use the conceptual distinction of Elazar 1988). This approach has an explicit anti-centralizing bias because it fragments sovereignty between distinct institutional entities, rather than transferring a chosen amount of general sovereignty from one level (the member state) to a higher level (the union). But it also has an explicit anti-differentiating bias because it affirms the necessity to preserve, across the board, the authority of the union in the fields in which the latter is sovereign.

That authority does not coincide with a government as in federal parliamentary states. If the European Parliament becomes the only institution that legitimates the European executive, then it is easy for large states to end up dominating small states. At the same time, that authority cannot have the intergovernmental characteristics that the Eurozone took on during the euro crisis. Asymmetric and differentiated unions of states are necessarily organized according to the logic of the vertical and horizontal separation of powers. In a union of states, there cannot be a central authority that incorporates the authorities of the states that make up that union, nor can there be a government as the institution of last resort. The US and Swiss experiences show us that unions of states can form and consolidate only if they abstain from becoming a state and from requiring a government for functioning. What justifies the formation of a federal union is not to overcome the territorial and institutional limits of the nation states that make it up, thus creating a super-state, albeit federal, which encapsulates those nation states. Nor can that union be established if it is only the expression of a European people (singular) that has already been formed or could be formed.

The Madisonian solution, based on a constitutional or political compact, implies the construction of powerful institutional firewalls between the national and supranational levels. Here there is no space for institutions fusing national and supranational polities. According to this view of federalization, member state sovereignties and federal sovereignty are not zero-sum correlated. One can prosper close to the other on the condition of constitutionally distinguishing between their respective competences. For instance, the European minister of finance should take care of European economic policy, manage a European treasury or fiscal capacity, and be accountable to European democratic institutions. Several authors (Enderlein and Haas 2015; European Commission 2015; Schauble 2012) have proposed that the European minister of finance, wearing the two hats of president of the ECOFIN Council and vice president of the Commission, should coordinate national economic policies. However, in the Madisonian perspective that minister should, instead, act autonomously within their own set of policy functions and responsibilities, leaving national economic policies to the responsibility of national democratic electorates and institutions. In concluding a very accurate analysis of the euro crisis, Henning (2017: 249) argued that, if the euro area had its own fiscal union with "a finance minister (administering) a euro-area budget," then "sovereign crises would become less likely, and when they did occur, financial assistance would be organized within the regular fiscal framework."

Whereas the solution to Rodrik's trilemma would lead toward further centralization, thus increasing the fusion between levels of government, Madison's approach would instead lead to drawing clear distinctions between the policies that fall under national or supranational institutions, thus preventing diffusion of a crisis from one to another level. Whereas the solution to Majone's dilemma would lead toward further differentiation, thus disintegrating the union as a democratically accountable organization, Madison's approach would instead lead to drawing a clear distinction between economic and political projects of integration. Indeed, the governance model elaborated in the previous chapter might offer a more promising answer to the question of how to organize a federal union in Europe.

The Political Nature of Federal Unions

The experience of the US (and that of Switzerland) gives us some methodological indications to reflect on the future of the EU. These are methodological because it is not a question of copying the US or Swiss experience, but of understanding the method used in those experiences to face dilemmas similar to those that the Europeans aiming at a political union with federal features will have to face (Fabbrini 2008: ch. 6). Federal unions are political compacts. They do not grow organically, nor can they emerge out of expediency or necessity. As Hamilton (now in Beard 1948: 137) argued in *Federalist Paper No. 35*, "Necessity, especially in politics, often occasions false hope, false reasoning and a system of measures, correspondently erroneous." Federal unions do not emerge from an evolutionary process, but instead from a political decision that identifies (or negotiates) the powers and competences of the union, leaving all the rest to the states constituting it. This is just the opposite of what has been conceptualized by the neo-functional and liberal intergovernmentalism approaches (for a discussion of the impact of the crises on those approaches, see Schimmelfennig 2018).

According to the neo-functionalist approach, which underlines the preeminent role of supranational actors in advancing integration, the latter depends on the transfer of policy responsibilities from the national to the supranational level. The new policy responsibilities, if well used, will help resolve collective problems, thus encouraging a corresponding transfer of loyalty on the part of national citizens toward the European institutions and authorities. According to this approach, crises can be an excellent opportunity to deepen the integration process by transferring competences and solutions to a supranational level, as argued by Jean Monnet himself (and Robert Schuman, as we have seen). Nonetheless, the multiple post-Lisbon Treaty crises have called into question this assumption (Fabbrini 2016b) and its political corollary. Supranational integration does not appear to be the inevitable outcome of the organismic development of the collaboration between states managed by supranational actors. As Brunnermeier, James, and Landau (2016: 33) observed, "The old Monnet mechanism of using crises to integrate Europe further seemed no longer to work. States, with their own fiscal capacity, looked more and more as if they were the backstop for confidence." The multiple crises of the 2010s have, in fact, led to a strengthening of the inter-governmental and not the supranational logic, an intergovernmental logic that, in turn, has increased the divisions between the member states in policy fields that are traditionally at the heart of national sovereignty. Likewise, the liberal intergovernmental approach, which underlines the preeminent role of national governments in advancing integration, has not emerged unscathed from the multiple crises of the 2010s. This approach considers integration as the outcome of the delivering of public goods satisfying national societal needs. If the main economic groupings in the individual states will benefit from the integration, then national consent would follow on deepening cooperation, thus incentivizing national governments to assign to supranational authorities the responsibility for implementing their economic decisions. This idea, however, does not consider the fact that integration of core state powers can favor some groups and pena-lize others. In addition, it does not consider that the relationship between citizens and integration is conditioned not only by economic interests, but also by their political or ideological vision. Just consider that in the United Kingdom, although the majority voted to leave the EU in the referendum of June 23, 2016, the main economic and business associations and the most influential social organizations had come out clearly in favor of the country staying in. Both analytical frames and corresponding narratives assume that integration is an organismic, inclu-sive, and growing process, driven by either supranational or national actors. Both narratives share a teleological assumption according to which the process of integration might be politically but not structurally constrained. Indeed, they never engaged in a serious discussion of the policies that should be managed at the supranational level and those at the national level of politics, because of their bias toward a centralizing outcome. The result was that, in the Europe of multiple crises, a formidable tension was activated between the two levels of government, a tension that led to a weakening of both national and supranational democracy.

An alternative paradigm, based on the comparative experience of democratic federations, is necessary. Historically, federal unions are the outcome of a political decision that clearly distributes powers and competences to both the center and the units. Instead of pressuring for the abstract transfer of sovereignty to the supranational level or for monitoring the practical delivery of the intergovernmental decision-making process, it would be necessary to clearly establish the confines and the form of the supranational authority. It is necessary to start from above, not from below, in thinking toward a democratic federal union. Only through a political decision is it possible to contain the fear of national governments of losing power and the ambition of supranational actors of extending their power. This is why it is necessary to free the concept of political union from its ambiguity and to interpret it as (precisely) a federal union. The latter, indeed, can escape the statist cage that immobilizes both parliamentary and intergovernmental perspectives on the political union. A European federal union can emerge only through a founding decision, not through a cumulative process. "Founding" here means identifying the limits within which both national and supranational authority should operate and the pieces of sovereignty allocated to each of them.

In this regard, the US experience is methodologically useful. The American states negotiated a (first) constitution (the Articles of Confederation of 1781) with which they tried to start a form of cooperation between themselves, military and economic, in an institution (the Continental Congress) with both executive and legislative functions. This constitution, however, did not work. The Continental Congress had taken on the characteristics of a diplomatic forum in which the states, represented as such, found it difficult to make collective decisions. Convened in Philadelphia in 1787, the state delegates matured the idea that they could not limit themselves to amending the existing constitution, but instead that it was necessary to draw up a new one. Thus, by going beyond the mandate they had received, the celebrated founding fathers of that country realized de facto a genuine coup d'état (Ellis 2015), because they agreed to change the nature of the political regime. This change then received the subsequent approval of constitutional conventions elected for this sole purpose in each of the member states of the new federation. The new (second) constitution was considered approved when it received the support of nine of the thirteen states of the Confederation, thus neutralizing the power of veto that had been a feature of the previous constitution. The new constitution did a lot more than transform the confederation into a federation. It created a federal union out of a pure exercise of political will by state political leaders. And this federal union was meant to avoid the possibility that on the new continent there might be formed a system of interstate cooperation unable to guarantee reciprocal security and to neutralize the dangers of domination of some states over other states. Between the formation of a new Westphalian state at the continental level and of an old confederacy of independent states, the US moved in the direction of an original experiment of aggregation of states based on the practice of divided sovereignty. Divided sovereignty cannot be reconciled with the idea of the federal nation state (assumed to be the only depository of sovereignty), nor with the idea of a confederacy of nation states (where each confederated state maintains its full sovereignty). The different states (in demographic and cultural terms) that started the process of aggregation would never accept joining a centralized organization endowed with a general authority that would claim superiority over the particular authorities represented by them. For this reason, the US is a federal union structured around a multiple separation of powers that, in order to function, requires neither a state nor a government. In this way, it was possible to combine the diversity of the federated states with the unity of the federal union. The US thus started from a purely political act, a political decision made by state elites and enshrined in a written constitution.

If it begins with a political pact between the leaders of different states, a federal union cannot presuppose the preexistence of a common identity between the citizens of those states, nor could it expect to build a common identity through the functioning of a preexistent state. A federal union should express a *pluribus* aiming to operate as an *unum*. However, the predominant predisposition among national political leaders and EU officials continues to be that of interpreting a political union on the basis of two models or myths

(Fabbrini 2010; Greenfeld 2012; Spruyt 1994), both aiming to a *pluribus* becoming an *unum*. Because in the French historical experience the formation of the state has preceded that of the nation and of democracy, anyone returning to this model has held that the EU would not have a future unless transformed into a state, so much so that the Constitutional Treaty was rejected in the French referendum of 2005 because it was inadequate to build the European institutional structure needed to control the market and protect citizens. For the French socialist leader Laurent Fabius, who led the campaign against the Constitutional Treaty in the referendum of May 2005, a lot more was needed if the desire was to build a new European statehood. Only a strong European public authority could create European citizenship, defending it at the same time from market interests. For the French experience, the existence of a European state is the necessary condition for generating a European people. The German experience was very different from the French. Prevented from forming a territorial state, but at the same time threatened by the expansionist tendency of the French territorial state, the German elites had to invent a cultural nation, a *demos*, to protect themselves from the expansionist aims of the bordering territorial state. Thus, unlike France, Germany had to construct a people in order to then build a state. This is an assumption that took root in the culture of that country, almost becoming orthodoxy. For example, for the German Federal Constitutional Court, the EU cannot integrate further until there is a European *demos*. And only when the latter shares a common identity will it then be possible to transfer competences and powers to Brussels, i.e., to construct a European political entity interpreted as a European federal state.[1]

Neither of these experiences is of any use to the European federal union. Because this union must aggregate asymmetric states in terms of population and differentiated in terms of national identity, it can neither accommodate a centralization of decision-making power nor build itself on the existence of a European people. Europe has many *demoi* that cannot and must not be streamed into a single *demos* (Nicolaidis 2013). A union of states must maintain the pluralism of national identities and the languages and cultural traditions of its

[1] This vision characterized the German Constitutional Court, from the decision of Maastricht-Urteil of 1993 (relating to the constitutionality of the Treaty of Maastricht) to the decisions of 2012 on the constitutionality of the Fiscal Compact and European Stability Mechanism.

citizens, even if it must encourage reciprocal knowledge, a condition necessary for mutual respect and tolerance. The point is that democratic unions of states cannot be based on a common cultural identity. They add a new (political) identity to the existing (national) identities. In the case of different languages, such unions encourage the sharing of a common language (which, in our case, must be English, a nationally neutral language because the United Kingdom will never be part of a federal union) that is added to the various national languages without usurping them. It is true that, after sixty years of integration, the distinct national identities have acquired many common characteristics to configure a kind of community of Europeans (Risse 2010). However, a federal union arises from the necessity to compound different national identities without threatening their individual persistence. The federal union is the response to the need to reconcile what appears impossible to reconcile, creating the conditions for the (eventual) melting of those national differences.

Federal unions should acknowledge national diversity among their member states, in addition to their similarities. Such diversity must be compounded, as already encapsulated in the motto of the EU (*in varietate concordia*). If a state or a people cannot hold a federal union together, where does the glue for such a union reside? The comparative analysis of federal unions (of the US and Switzerland) has led us to a single response: That glue resides in the constitution. A federal union of asymmetrical and differentiated states requires a founding pact between its members to establish the purely political reasons of the aggregation project. The political compact defines the basic rules of the game and the basic principles to be respected, for both the institutions and the citizens who operate within them. The form of the pact can vary, but its nature as a political pact (and not a cultural pact based on ethnic or religious affinities) cannot be denied. Because they do not share a common identity, in the US the federated states have built a constitutional system that guarantees their specific identities. Because they have irreconcilable cultural (if not national) divisions, they have entrusted to the constitution the task of defining a political identity as the only one that could be universally acceptable to everyone. Particularly after the Civil War of 1861–1865, the Constitution (with its political universalism) became the source of political American identity, the text of a kind of civil religion of the country.

Certainly, not everyone agreed with this vision. Indeed, immediately after the Philadelphia Convention, political movements developed that were angrily engaged to defend a presumed original identity of the country (that of the so-called White Anglo-Saxon Protestants, who were held to be the founders of the "new nation"). From the Alien and Sedition Acts of 1798 (a set of four laws used to deny citizenship to foreigners; anyone who criticized the country was pursued in the criminal courts and the president was given the power to expel any foreigner who was considered dangerous, of which three were then abrogated a few years later) to the entry into the White House in January 2017 of the ideologists of white supremacy with the presidency of Donald Trump, the nativistic vision has never been scared off. The more the policy of openness and inclusion has been successful, the more the nativistic reaction has made itself felt. The democratic history of the US has been accompanied by a permanent battle between the promotors of a political (and thus multiple) identity and the defenders of a cultural (and thus unique) identity of the country. However, the supporters of political union have had a formidable instrument available to them: the Constitution. The idea is that only the Constitution and its political values (and not the national culture or the ethnic origin or the native language, as argued, among others, by Huntington 2004) can keep the union together. The clash between the two visions is not similar to a gala dinner. After all, if in a democracy nothing can be considered as acquired forever, in a compound democracy this is even truer because of the very complexity and diversity of the federal union that it organizes. In short, federal unions emerge from a political decision and develop thanks to a political identity. The Constitution is the glue that unites states and citizens who are different in terms of cultural identities and distinct in terms of regional interests (Walzer 1996). It is the glue and not the cage. Public institutions transformed themselves dramatically along the course of US history, but it was a transformation within the constitutional frame and not outside of it. The Constitution is the strongbox in which to deposit sovereignty. It provides the language and procedures for regulating the contradictions that make up a federal union, because it should be a system open to the formation of changing equilibria between the center and the states, as well as between the executive and the legislature. Sovereignty is therefore deposited in the Constitution, not in the federated states or in the federal center. This is the Madisonian solution to the paradox of reconciling sovereign states within a sovereign union (Fabbrini 2008).

If the analysis developed in this book is of any help, then it is unlikely that the political transformation of the EU into a federal union will be shared by states that have systematically claimed an opt-out from crucial policies or have hampered the deepening of integration in the name of their overriding economic vision of integration. The acknowledgment of this impossibility constitutes the crucial step to be taken by those sharing the political perspective of integration.

From Differentiation to Decoupling

It may be argued that the multiple crises, Brexit, the control of government by sovereignist parties in eastern Europe, the growing influence of sovereignist movements in western and southern Europe, and the changes in the transatlantic equilibria will not produce radical alterations in the European geo-political situation. The crises are going to be overcome, the economic recovery will reduce the sovereignist pressure, Brexit should not be overstated given it is the expression of the idiosyncrasies of an island, and the US neo-nationalism cannot structurally last for too long. If this is the case, then, within the unitary legal order of the EU, a strategy may be pursued for preserving the current governance framework. However, the neutralization of sovereignist challenges requires much more than business as usual. In fact, this strategy would contribute to increasing dissatisfaction on the part of those who support the EU (because of the ineffectiveness of the policies pursued), without winning over the consensus of those who are instead against the EU (because they do not recognize its legitimacy). The diffusion and radicalization of sovereignist sentiments cannot be addressed proposing the old combination of policies or hiding the integration's aims. Certainly, the force of administrative inertia, the resistance of bureaucratic interests, and the short-termism of politics must not be underestimated. The pressure to go on as before is not only substantial but also institutionalized. Yet, sovereignism can be defeated only by a bold vision of Europe's future, not by the defense of existing procedures or by a "to do" list (Merritt 2016: 229).

If one accepts the argument that the EU policy differentiation, making inefficient its functioning and opaque its legitimacy, has contributed to the growth of popular dissatisfaction against the European integration project, then a strategy of continuity cannot be justifiable. If the consequences of the multiple crises are recognized, with their triggering of sovereignist movements and parties, and if the geopolitical changes are not at all transient, then it is necessary to think of a strategy of discontinuity, for the very reason that being radically discontinuous (compared with the past) is the condition in which the EU finds itself. This strategy aims to decouple the current EU into two organizations, an economic community and a political union, thus organizing the latter according to the federal union's model. This strategy requires a double preliminary act to be agreed on by national and European leaders, a first act for distinguishing the political and the economic projects of integration and a second act for defining the nature of the political project. In the latter case, a statement of political intent (a political compact) should be signed by the leaders of a group of countries who plausibly represent the members of the Eurozone (but probably not all of them), a commitment to move toward a federal union operating within the single market as the organization open to all the European states (as to the old non-members of the EU, as Norway, and the new non-members of the EU, as the United Kingdom). The political statement should then lead to a redefinition of the governance model of an "ever closer union." It is not possible to return to the experience of the Constitutional Convention of Brussels of 2002–2003, with the vetoes and influence-mongering that characterized it. It is rather a question, between the leaders of both national governments and EU institutions, of agreeing on the possibility of starting a process of constitutional differentiation for creating two organizations based on distinct legal orders, despite living within the same economic condominium. This negotiated agreement would benefit both those who want or need to set up a political union and those who desire or need to participate only in an economic community. Without that preliminary political act, it is unlikely that this strategy would lead to a constitutionally defined federal union. This strategy, it might be noted, would theoretically connect, giving them distinct governance forms, the second and fourth scenarios devised by the 2017 Commission's white paper, with the second scenario ("nothing but the single market") as the inclusive economic community and the fourth scenario ("doing less more efficiently") as the exclusive federal union.

Of course, this strategy too would face numerous problems, of both a procedural and an institutional nature. The procedural problem concerns the first step to be taken for starting a process for politically separating a core of Eurozone member states from those interested only in the functioning of the single market. If the rhetoric on a united Europe within a single framework is abandoned and there is an agreement on the fact that it is possible to answer differently to different needs and perspectives maintaining a common economic and security basis, then these problems can be pragmatically resolved. The institutional problem concerns the engineering of carving out the institutional framework of the federal union from the current institutional framework of the EU. It is not advisable to create new institutions because that would unnecessarily increase complexity. It is rather plausible to organize the relations differently between the existing institutions for the different purposes they have to pursue. As shown in Chapter 4, the multiple separation of powers of the federal union's governance can be realized through a reform of the existing dual executive and bicameral legislature, while the economic community's governance can be guaranteed by different combinations and different powers of the same institutions. Creativity is the resource required for bringing the integration's project to deal with the need of its decoupling.

The decoupling of the Lisbon Treaty resides in a negotiation that should generate a positive-sum outcome because it would allow the creation of different institutional spaces for different integration strategies or needs. A plural Europe should be based on a political pact between the countries of the Eurozone (or the core of it) and an economic pact between the latter and the other countries that are part of (or want to be part only of) the single market. The two pacts must be capable of differentiation on the legal level, because they aim to meet distinct needs. However, the countries that sign them must maintain a solid link within the regulatory framework of the single market. At the same time, the political pact should lead to redefinition of the governance framework, moving toward a federal union. If the political union should be a "federation of nation states" (to use Jacques Delors's words), then the latter's differences and rivalries can be reconciled only by a system of multiple separation of powers regulated by a political pact enshrined in a fundamental charter. The constitutional pact (or political compact) should be the depositary of the federal union sovereignty, not of the member state sovereignties that are enshrined in their national constitutions. The multiple separation of powers can make it possible to keep in the same organization large and small states, states with strong and weak institutional configurations, states with diverse national identities.

The European federal union does not come into being with the task of replacing national democracies with a supranational democracy, nation states with a supranational state, national peoples with a supranational people. As with other federal unions, the European federal union should be a compound polity because it accommodates national democracies with the supranational democracy, distinguishing the policies that are subject to the control of the former and those subject to the governance of the latter. It should be the opposite of what has been created in the intergovernmental Eurozone, where it is increasingly difficult to distinguish national and European competences, national and European responsibilities, in accordance with a logic that, by fusing the levels of government, prevents the distinction of responsibility in their functioning. But it should also be different from a parliamentary union with its fusion of horizontal powers that would increase the influence of the larger states on the smaller states. Through the separation of national democracies from supranational democracy, and the separation of institutions of the latter, it will then be possible to reduce anti-Europeanism. Sovereignism has been in fact fed by the frustration of citizens at an integration process that prevents them from influencing choices made at the European level, choices that nevertheless affect their national condition.

If the European federal union wants to be a union between equals, then it is necessary to move toward a governance system that prevents the formation of hierarchies between its member states and that encourages decision-making processes based on checks and balances between institutions. These are aims that only the separation of powers, mitigated by appropriate mechanisms, can pursue. Of course, such a governance system complicates the decision-making process, making possible stalemate and contrast between institutions. Nonetheless, original expedients can be identified to reduce its dysfunctions (such as proposed, for example, by Cain 2015 with reference to the US experience). However, even the most effective of these expedients can do little if are used by political elites unaware of the fragility of a federal union, thus willing to make compromises between the member states and between the institutions of the separation of powers. Federal unions are condemned to live the daily miracle of functioning without a people, a government, and a state (Fabbrini 2010).

It is true that the EU has become a highly differentiated organization; it is also true that such differentiation has led the EU into a constitutional conundrum (Fabbrini 2016d). Moving from policy differentiation to constitutional decoupling can free the EU from opacity, hierarchy, or stalemate. To avoid conceptual overstretching, it would be more appropriate to talk of a plural, rather than differentiated, Europe in the case of constitutional decoupling. Two organizations must be able to form, each of which is engaged in pursuing different ends, on the basis of differing agreements, even if then reciprocally linked in what unites them, the single market as well as the military alliance of NATO. The first organization is the exclusive federal union, based on a political agreement of constitutional import, built starting from the core member states of the Eurozone. The second organization is the inclusive economic community, open to all the European states that respect the basic principles of the rule of law and the fundamental criteria of the free market, based on an essential and functional interstate treaty.

The economic community does not call into question national sovereignty as regards core state powers, although it should equip itself with a basic supranational framework to regulate the single market and resolve disputes between its state and economic actors. On the contrary, the federal union implies a division of sovereignty between national and supranational levels of government. For this reason, the latter must celebrate the political reasons for its creation, while this is not necessary for setting up the former. A single market can function without the existence of a common currency, just as participation in such a market does not require sharing foreign, military, or security policy or management of home affairs (which are instead crucial powers of the federal union). Of course, a single market does not even imply the existence of redistributive policies (such as structural funds) that presuppose a solidarity-based sharing of its function. Those policies can be promoted in exchange for other shared policies (such as that on immigration), but this must be part of negotiations between the members of the federal union and the other states that participate in the economic community. Nothing will be due without reciprocity. Certainly, it is necessary to define the role of the federal union within the economic community, introducing institutional expedients that can prevent the formation of a blocking majority of the former within the latter.

Conclusion

To weaken the "holy" alliance between populism and nationalism, it is necessary to free the EU from the tyranny of "one size fits all," to distinguish institutionally between the countries that need to move toward political integration and those that wish to participate only in a single market. Recognizing the legitimate right of the latter to preserve their national sovereignty, but involving them in the single market, would help to keep their nationalism under control. At the same time, institutionalizing a distinct federal union (around the Eurozone member states), governing traditional core state powers through a separation of power system, would certainly help undermine the populism fomented by inefficient and illegitimate intergovernmental governance. The single market and the federal union should have different institutional settings, although the member states of the latter would participate in the functioning of the former, according to rules that would prevent them acting en bloc.

Consequently, the federal union that should be built in Europe will be *smaller*, but also *more united*, than the current EU. It will be smaller, but not small, because, if it corresponds to the current Eurozone, it will represent around 330 million inhabitants (a higher number than the US), compared with more than 440 million inhabitants of the EU without the United Kingdom. Nonetheless, if the economic community also includes other European states disposed to economic cooperation and that are currently not members of the EU (such as Norway, Switzerland, and, looking forward, the Balkan states and a re-democratized Turkey) and manages to once again involve the United Kingdom, then the relations, in the single market, between the countries of the federal union and the countries that are not part of it will be much more balanced. The federal union will be more united, but not centralized, held together by a political pact of constitutional weight that should prevent fusion or confusion of powers. Such a federal union would be a bulwark against sovereignism, showing that it is possible to be part of a federal project without depleting national democratic institutions, without losing national cultural identities, or without giving up legitimate national interests. Its existence would therefore be a factor of stabilization for the whole continent. If it expands, those joining must explicitly accept the constitutional pact on which it is based. And, once joined, those states should know that secession will be constitutionally impossible. Nonetheless, it is possible to be part of an economically integrated Europe without necessarily being part of a politically integrated Europe.

The future thus resides in a plural Europe constituted by an (enlarged) economic community open to all the states of the continent, as well as to those that thus far have not joined the EU or that had previously decided to leave it, and a (smaller) federal union operating within that economic community. The model of the federal union is the only realistic response to the question concerning distinct identities and different demographic sizes within a supranational project. The strategy for building the federal union acknowledges that nation states cannot be abolished, but it assumes that they can be brought within a constitutional context balancing their power through multiple (horizontal and vertical) institutional separations. In a federal union, national democracies are not depleted, but preserved (and even strengthened), keeping them separated from the supranational democracy. The European federal union requires a new political thought to valorize the differences between states and their citizens, to constitutionalize the separations of responsibilities between the levels of government, and, above all, to free the aggregation from centralizing and statist tendencies. A new science of integration is necessary for thinking about Europe's future.

Conclusion: Two Organizations in a Plural Europe

Introduction

The "holy" alliance between populism and nationalism has led to the re-affirmation of the principle of national sovereignty (*sovereignism*) because of the institutional weakness of the integration process. Certainly, nationalist populism in western Europe has been fed by social inequalities that the governance of the Eurozone has not only not regulated but has also heightened (Matthijs 2017), or been fed by badly managed migration and security policies. Instead, the populist nationalism of eastern Europe has been fed mainly by the challenges in terms of identity produced by mass migration that EU governance has not only not governed, but that is considered to be the cause of its explosion. The multiple crises have been due to objective factors, such as speculation on finance markets, irresponsible policies in managing national budgets, and mass movements of populations to escape hardship or wars, but their effects have been amplified by the inadequacy of the institutional system designed to govern those factors. This inadequacy is the result of interstate compromises that have proved insufficient compared with the challenges to be faced. Those compromises have prevented the EU from acting effectively and legitimately, thus feeding the ill ease that is used by populists and nationalists. In addition, those compromises have differentiated the EU internally, but without weakening the orthodoxy that has continued to defend the principle that the integration process must continue to be unitary and inclusive. However, there cannot be just one solution for different situations. The idea of one size fits all (as Schmidt 2016 argued) has ended up producing uncertain policies, which for some are too limited and for others are too invasive. This is all to the benefit of sovereignists who, after Brexit, seem engaged in hollowing out the EU from within rather than leaving it altogether.

If anti-elitism is a recurrent sentiment of liberal democracies, then the governance of the Eurozone and of the EU has given the sovereignist sentiment new reasons to spread. Of course, not all the countries of the Eurozone have been affected in the same way by the centralizing degeneration of its governance model. In countries such as Germany, which is comfortable with the ordo-liberal model and even more so with its intergovernmental management, the sovereignist reaction has been significant but limited, with the electoral affirmation of the *Alternative für Deutschland* (AfD) getting 12.6 percent of the votes in the September 24, 2017, parliamentary elections. In countries such as Italy and France, on the other hand, where their political economies are barely reconcilable with the ordo-liberal model, the popular reaction against the management of the Eurozone has been overwhelming. In France, in the first round of the presidential elections held on April 23, 2017, the two main anti-EU candidates (Marine Le Pen and Jean-Luc Mélenchon) together got 40 percent of the votes; and in Italy, in the parliamentary elections of March 4, 2018, the two main anti-EU parties (Five Star Movement and League) got more than 50 percent of the votes (and formed a sovereignist government). In short, populism, which is natural to liberal democracies, has ended up becoming, in the integrated Europe of the single currency, a political support of sovereignism. At the same time, the strengthening of the intergovernmental approach in policy areas of vital importance for national governments and electorates has increased the rivalry and divergences among member states. Here, I proceed as follows: First, I wrap up the analysis of the intergovernmental governance, interpreting it as a post-democratic experience. Second, I synthetize the argument of this book, namely, the need to decouple the EU into a federal union within an economic community. Third, and finally, I conclude by returning to the Ventotene Manifesto that inaugurated, in 1941, the modern thought on European integration.

Intergovernmentalism as Post-democracy

The uncertainty of the EU in dealing with the euro crisis, the arrival in Europe of a massive number of political refugees and economic migrants, and thus the terrorist attacks on the civilian population in European cities can be considered co-responsible for the rise of anti-Europeanism across all EU member states. That uncertainty has been the result not only of the magnitude of the challenges but also of the lack of legitimacy of the intergovernmental system, particularly when it operates in conditions of crises. Decisions with highly distributive effects have been made without the democratic inputs of the citizens affected by them. The mismatch between intergovernmental decisions and democratic politics could not fail to generate a popular reaction, specifically in those member states that encountered more structural and cultural difficulties in adjusting to the ordo-liberal model of the Eurozone. It is not a matter of justifying who has governed badly in the past. Far from it. However, the model of convergence, if not of uniformity, between national policies celebrated by the ordo-liberal theory and protected by the intergovernmental constitution (and by the pacts and treaties that strengthened it), ended up favoring some countries and penalizing others. This provoked the popular reaction against policies perceived as the outcome of decisions made by supranational technocracies (from the European Commission to the other independent agencies), but which were instead made by national governments, thus entrusting those technocrats to implement them. It is necessary to point out the bad faith of many national political leaders who contribute to making decisions in Brussels and then criticize those decisions when they are back in their national capitals. However, the problem is structural, not just behavioral. It is due to the idea that economic convergence should proceed only from below, through national structural reforms aiming to make the national fiscal budget sustainable. Indeed, in a union of asymmetric and differentiated states, convergence should also be promoted from above through the use of independent budgetary resources to use for investing in common projects or for neutralizing the negative effects of the economic cycle. However, even during the worst days of the euro crisis, no one had the courage to give the Eurozone its own budget and its own system of democratic government, with the result that the decisions were made through mediation among nineteen national governments in a political climate of reciprocal distrust – a distrust that asked for periodical rules to keep it under control. Of course, a rule-based system of economic governance is politically irresponsible. Indeed, the citizens dissatisfied with the Eurozone's decisions ended up voting down domestic incumbent governments, notwithstanding none of them was singularly responsible for the decisions collegially made.

This is true not only for economic policies, but also for other inter-governmental policies that are sensitive for national governments, such as that on immigration. In this case, too, there is no common European migration policy. Each member state claims its own autonomy in accepting the outcome of collective deliberation to which, however, it contributes. Thus, in managing a policy that has significant domestic implications, the interest of individual national governments may conflict with the interest of other individual national governments. Each national leader thinks about their own reelection or the next electoral deadline. Thus, the immigration of millions of people into Europe (a fact of history) was addressed by the various national governments on the basis of specific electoral calculations (a fact of contingent importance). The EU's inability to manage this massive flow of people into European countries (and into some of them in particular) has ended up justifying the populist mobilization with its clear (but ineffective) request to shut down national borders. Nationalist sentiments have found fertile ground in threats to the identity of citizens. It has been the inadequacy of a migration policy based on agreement among the national governments that has exasperated the problem. After all, how could it have been conceived to build an area for the free circulation of people among member states of the EU (the so-called Schengen area) without having planned at the same time for a common protection of the borders of that area? It is the same logic institutionalized in the Eurozone: a common currency without a common budget managed by a common authority. National governments have strenuously defended the principle that it is their duty to control their own territory, even if this principle is empirically contradicted by their inability in ensuring that control. And yet, despite the repeated waves of immigrant arrivals that have occurred since the start of the 2010s, the EU has not managed to come up with a supranational policy to manage immigration. The Dublin Agreements are still in force (albeit revised several times), on the basis of which it is the responsibility of the country of first arrival to handle the registration and management of immigrants, with penalizing (economic and organizational) effects for some countries but not for others. Only at the end of 2016 was a small step taken with the strengthening of Frontex, the European border and coastal control agency – a small step, because its duty remains that of supplementing national border agencies where necessary, but not of guaranteeing (independently from the national agencies) protection from outside the area of free internal circulation.

Migration policy has confirmed the paradox of intergovernmental integration. There is no European policy on immigration owing to the resistance of member states that want to preserve sovereignty over their national territory. However, those countries are not capable of guaranteeing that sovereignty given the size of the migratory phenomenon. Thus, the absence of a European immigration policy increases citizens' feeling of dissatisfaction toward the EU, accused of being insensitive to the fears and insecurity that immigration produces in national societies – all in all, a real disaster. While wishing to preserve national sovereignty over migration policy (territorial sovereignty) as well as over economic policy (fiscal sovereignty), but because there are conflicts between those sovereignties, reciprocal mistrust between those sovereignties has led either to policy stalemate or to the empowerment of technocratic agencies. In short, responsibility for the decision-making shortfalls of the intergovernmental model is transferred to the European technocracies, with the Commission having to play the bad cop role to make up for those decision-making shortfalls. In the Eurozone, the Commission has felt both the dissatisfaction of citizens from debtor countries owing to its excessive rigidity in enforcing the rules and the dissatisfaction of citizens from creditor countries for not being rigid enough in enforcing those rules. And it is against the Commission that the anger of the governments of eastern Europe has been directed for having proposed a system of allocating national quotas of political refugees and the anger of the governments of southern Europe for not having done enough to lighten the burden of handling the refugees who have landed on their coasts. The result has been that, while those technocracies (such as the Commission) have sought to do their best to make a virtue out of a vice by preserving a European interest in a context where national visions and ambitions have held sway, citizens have directed toward these technocrats their ill ease due to the decision-making system that their governments have built in Brussels. It is worth recalling that, in a crisis situation, taking just a half step forward can upset both those who wanted to take a full step and those who would prefer to stay put.

In the context of crises that have distributive effects, the intergovernmental model does not create consensus among national governments, but instead worsens the differences between them. Large countries such as Germany think that the intergovernmental model fully satisfies their interests, because it does not generate a mismatch between domestic politics and European choices. These countries have managed to transfer to the Eurozone their internal constraints, both those from the political system (symbolized by the role of their national parliaments) and those from the legal system (symbolized by the role of their constitutional courts) (Bulmer 2014). It is not the same for other countries of the Eurozone. In debtor countries and in those structured around a political economy inconsistent with the ordo-liberal logic, constraints have operated in the opposite way, from the Eurozone to domestic politics. This has had the effect of de-structuring the internal political system of the latter countries, because they have shown the ineffectiveness of that system compared with the logic of how the Eurozone operates. This is also true for other important domestic policies, such as migration policy. Facing decisions with enormous domestic impacts, the asymmetry between national governments that are coordinated in the European Council or in the Councils of Ministers has created real hierarchies of power. Politics as the struggle for the power to decide has crept back in through the window of the European Council, after an attempt was made to boot it out by the same in celebrating the consensual nature of its deliberations. However, if the intergovernmental model can meet the interests of the largest countries in the short term, in the medium term it can damage the system that has protected those interests so far. Indeed, the de-structuring of the internal political systems of the weaker countries or those with political economies that cannot be reconciled with the ordo-liberal approach is leading to the electoral strengthening of sovereignist movements (as happened in Italy). This is making it possible for the leaders of nationalist populism to take control of the respective national governments and so participate in intergovernmental governance. Because the European Council is considered an institution that is self-centered, that is, an institution that does not require checks and balances at the EU level (i.e., from the European Parliament), the sovereignist (national) leaders, by becoming the majority in that Council, can undermine the integration process from within, watering down its supranational (i.e., suprastate) features and orienting it toward the Europe of the homelands (i.e., an international organization based on interstate relations). The member states that defend the political model of the intergovernmental union would do well to reflect more deeply on their national interest. They should ask themselves whether that interest really resides in an increasingly intergovernmental EU, internally divided, or in a reformed EU, according to the model of the federal union, that can prevent the sovereignist outcome. Remember: it would not be the first time in Europe that sleepwalking governments have headed blissfully toward the abyss (Clark 2014).

Habermas (2012) defined the system of intergovernmental governance as executive federalism. In terms of comparative institutional analysis, the definition does not stand up. Executive federalism recalls the Canadian experience in which a significant (informal) role in the decision-making process is played by the informal First Ministers' Conference involving the federal prime minister and the provincial prime ministers, or it recalls the German experience in which a formal role in policy making is played by the *Bundesrat*. Nonetheless, in both cases, there is an institution of political legitimization that is not controlled by the governments of the *Länder* or by the prime ministers of the Canadian provinces. Nothing of the kind can be found in the intergovernmental EU, where Brussels institutions of national governments monopolize the decision-making process without any check from other Brussels institutions (the European Parliament, in particular). The intergovernmental EU is removed not only from the various federal models but also from the various democratic models. Indeed, it has acquired the characteristics of a "post-democratic" system (Crouch 2004). In terms of political analysis, however, Habermas is right to argue that the intergovernmental logic is at the origin of the crisis of the EU. In the Eurozone, intergovernmental governance has ended up in building a centralized administrative system that recalls a "state without democracy."

Decoupling the European Union

To reform the EU means to move in the direction of its constitutional decoupling, between an economic community for managing (basic) single market policies and a federal union, constituted by member states needing or willing to create an "ever closer union" for governing strategic policies. The economic community should be based on a purely interstate treaty for regulating policies strictly necessary for the functioning of the single market. Its governance system can start from the current quadrilateral institutional system, although power and competences of the single institutions should be redefined and simplified. It would be nevertheless necessary to acknowledge, by each of the states participating in it, that a single market requires supranational authorities and rules for functioning and making it globally competitive (e.g., in international trade). The single market should preserve its founding principles of free circulation of individuals, goods, services, and capital (although their implementation should be sufficiently flexible to deal with extraordinary events). It should also imply the sharing of basic values and institutions of rule of law by its participants. At the same time, the federal union should be based on a constitutional pact (or political compact). A federal union is not a federal state, because of its anti-centralizing logic. Federal unions are based on the principle of divided sovereignty between the federal center and the federated states. Each of the two levels has sovereignty over the management of policies for which it is responsible and distinct democratic institutions are needed to implement the divided sovereignty. A federal union is a compound democracy in which the levels of national and supranational authorities are clearly separated. Thus, the single market must remain the defining and indispensable framework for the federal union and other less integrated forms of cooperation between member states. It is necessary to stop thinking that a union of states can become democratic only through the form of the federal state. A federal union implies the definition of the limited competences of the federal center, leaving all the rest to the federated states. A federal union is the opposite of both the EU and the Eurozone, characterized by the disorderly expansion of competences, in an institutional context of unclear lines of accountability. Although the policy competences of the federal union are limited, those policy competences exclude the possibility that one or another member state could opt out of them. A federal union's jurisdiction, in its policy domains, has (and should have) a general scope and a political pact should be sufficiently rigid to deal with centrifugal pressures.

At the same time, a federal union does not imply the existence of a single identity, as is implied historically in nation states (even federally, with the partial exception of Canada). In fact, the existence of an exclusive identity is the property of unitary organizations such as the state. In a federal union, it is not a question of transferring the identity or the loyalty of the citizens from the national to the European level, thus creating a European identity to replace the national identity. This single vision of identity, which continues to influence the most ardent supporters of European integration, is both effect and cause of the predominance of the statist paradigm in Europeanist public culture, a paradigm that requires the existence of a single and homogeneous *demos*. Europeanism (or, even less so, cosmopolitism) can provide identity to restricted intellectual or economic or public elites, but it cannot represent the goal for national citizenships. Between the exclusive national or European identity there is a broad area of multiple and diverse identities. For this reason, it is necessary to set up a federal union, not a federal state. A federal union is a compound organization, wherein citizens can cultivate their national identities and, at the same time, by dialoguing with the national identities of the other citizens can construct a new political identity at the European level. National identities are the outcome of cultural strategies pursued historically by elites aiming to reach precise political goals. Just like nations, identities too were invented. Thus, one cannot exclude that the process of Europeanization would end in changing them again. Nonetheless, from an analytical viewpoint, those national identities do exist – they are a reality to consider. As Judt (2005: 797) observed, "Over the course of the twentieth century the European nation-state took on considerable responsibilities for its citizens' welfare, security and well-being" that makes it unrealistic to discard the persistence of national identities. The federal union reflects a Europe of many *demoi*, of plural citizenships with differing national identities. The latter is a necessary condition to guarantee the pluralism of the union. The idea of erasing national identities is unrealistic besides being illiberal. Indeed, by not acknowledging their social legitimacy, statist federalism has ended up confusing national identities with nationalism, almost as if they were the same thing. But it is not so. National identity is inclusive and adaptable. Nationalism is exclusive and rigid. National identity is compatible with plurality. Nationalism may not be.

For this reason, to beat the "holy" alliance, it is necessary to build a federal union that can preserve, and at the same time mix, national identities. Only in this way will those identities not degenerate into nationalism, as has happened during the multiple crises of the 2010s as a result of the regulatory centralization that robbed national democracies of meaning. In a federal union, citizens can cultivate their multiple identities, while in federal states they are driven to having a single overarching identity. The institutions of the federal union must be separate, as are the identities of citizens. The community of Europeans (Risse 2010) must be made up of individuals with multiple identities, not with an exclusive supranational or cosmopolitan identity (on this, see also McNamara 2017). What unites Europeans must be a political pact, the adherence to political values, the respect for the procedures and institutions substantiating that pact. Only politics, and its democratic underpinning, can unite those diverse national identities. The historical error of Europeanism was that of wanting to build a European cultural identity to replace national cultural identities, as well as to build a European federal state to replace the various nation states. It is no coincidence that every attempt to unite Europeans culturally has produced exactly the opposite; it has divided them, because European pluralism can never be enclosed in a single cultural identity (recall the angry debate on the Preamble of the failed Constitutional Treaty during the Brussels convention of 2002–2003). The European identity can be only political, while national identities may continue to be cultural. Time and history will tell us the outcome of the interaction between the two. Keep in mind, moreover, that every attempt to centralize authority in Europe led historically to an increase in conflicts between states or groups of them. For this reason, the federal union needs a constitution on which not only to legitimate itself but also to limit its powers. A federal union is necessary for Europe, as well as for the countries that make it up. It helps to contain the nationalist urges within its member states, taking legitimate decisions on issues of common interest, without at the same time undermining national democracies because of invading policy areas that pertain to them. Moreover, a federal union, with its constitutional culture, is also a bulwark against illiberal sentiments emerging in the other states that are in the single market of the economic community.

Back to Ventotene

Europe needs to go back to Ventotene. Ventotene is the island where Altiero Spinelli and Ernesto Rossi, who had been detained by the Italian fascist regime, drafted (in June 1941) the *Manifesto for a Free and United Europe*. It is the island where thought was dedicated to the future of Europe while Europe was killing itself in a fratricidal war. Starting again from Ventotene means, today, developing a new idea of the future of Europe that is coherent with the spirit of that Manifesto, but which considers the deep changes that occurred during the subsequent eighty years. With the multiple crises of the 2010s, the integration project has been called into question, although disintegration as epitomized by Brexit does not seem to represent an alternative political pattern. Rather, the sovereignist forces, emerged during the crises, aim toward a transformation of the EU from within, a transformation into an organization of economic cooperation compatible with the preservation of national sovereignty in policy realms considered crucial by the incumbent national governments. As Parsons and Matthijs (2015: 210) asserted, "Until a coherent organizational vision and bold leadership return to champion it," it will be difficult to deal with the sovereignist challenge. A radically different approach is thus necessary to provide an innovative redefinition of both the narrative and the form of the Europe of tomorrow. In this book, I have tried to initiate a reflection on these points, which I now summarize by way of conclusion.

With respect to the narrative, we have seen that the integration project was justified at the start by an unequivocal aspiration: Stop wars among European states. It was then considered that the peace (which is guaranteed by NATO) would be all the more secure, the more it was accompanied by economic well-being, social welfare, and political freedoms (promoted by the EU). On these bases, integration went ahead, first, between the countries of western Europe and then the countries of southern and eastern Europe. This success did not prevent the EU from being engulfed in a series of crises. The goal of an inevitable move toward the United States of Europe was dramatically cut off at the knees by the outcome of the British referendum of June 23, 2016, and the uncontrolled spread of populism and nationalism. The EU's enlargement to include almost all the countries of the continent has increased its lack of internal homogeneity (heightening differences and suspicions). This lack of homogeneity, in the presence of crises with distributive effects managed through the intergovernmental constitution, has shown the difficulty in reconciling the various perspectives on integration pursued by its member states. In the crises, Europe has confirmed it is a plural continent, where countries with differing histories, interests, and identities interpret differently the need for transnational cooperation. Those national identities must be recognized for the systemic role that they play, that of representing the source of solidarity which is deeply rooted in the history of those countries. At the same time, however, they must be shorn of their antagonistic potential. A compound Europe cannot be organized by governance models expressing (in both their parliamentary or intergovernmental versions) a statist bias on the integration's finality. The increasing differentiation in Europe requires the elaboration of a narrative that is different from the past – a narrative not only to preserve and enhance what we have in common (the military alliance within NATO that should be strengthened and the single market that should increasingly expand to other European countries not yet part of it), but also to recognize the perspectives that differentiate the various EU member states. Different perspectives, nonetheless, must be developed within a shared liberal culture of open market and rule of law. A new narrative is necessary to explain the need for moving in the direction of a plural Europe, respecting the countries that do not wish to go beyond trans-national economic cooperation and at the same time enabling countries (such as most of those sharing the same currency) that need to move forward toward political integration. A federal union is the necessary condition for governing the single currency, for guaranteeing protection to its citizens, and for promoting European values and interests in a global world.

With respect to the form, if it is acknowledged that there are countries that want or need to move toward a federal (political) union and countries whose request is to take part only in an interstate (economic) community, then the shared policies to be pursued for the latter cannot be the same as those for the former. For the economic community, the basis should be an interstate agreement like the Single European Act of 1986, enriched by those policies that have been proved necessary for the operation of a single, open, and competitive market. An economic community requires competition policy but does not require the adoption of a common foreign or security policy, nor does it require a common policy for home affairs or immigration. It does not even require a single currency, once balanced exchange rates between the different currency regimes are established. For the federal union, instead, the challenge will be more complex. Here it is a question of creating a constitutionally anti-centralizing system, and yet capable of making legitimate and effective decisions, if organized according to the model of multiple separation of powers. A federal union does not imply the transfer of sovereignty from member states to the center. Rather, it is based on a division of sovereignty, distinguishing between the policies and resources that must remain national and the policies and resources that are shared at the supranational level. The federal union must have its own security and defense policy (with its own military and intelligence capabilities), its own home affairs and justice policy, its own immigration and border control policy. It is necessary to stress that a divided sovereignty does not prevent member states from having their own system of security, defense, intelligence, home affairs, or justice. It should be the mission of the constitution's negotiation to define who does what, when, and how. And obviously the federal union must have its own currency, connected to a budget policy supported by its own fiscal resources and not transferred from member states. In these policies, the central authority does not have delegated authority from the states, nor are the resources to manage its responsibilities dependent on the latter. Economic convergence between its member states is preferable, but it is not an essential condition for the existence of the union. A member state can fail without calling into question the viability of the whole union, if the latter has independent fiscal capacity and governance institutions to pursue anti-cyclical policies (if this is the will of the citizens who legitimate it in electoral terms). Finally, of course, it is necessary to establish the conditions for entering in the federal union (without the possibility of leaving it once entered) and for its members to act in the economic community of the single market.

Conclusion

If it is true that the EU is internally divided between countries with a political vision (or that need to move toward political aggregation) and others with an economic vision of integration, then it is barely plausible to believe that they can share the same institutional framework. If the desire is to disaggregate and integrate at the same time, then it is necessary to create two distinct legal and institutional orders. Of course, an economic community will also require the existence of supranational bodies to guarantee respect of the four fundamental economic freedoms in all the countries that are part of it. However, it is a question not only of light bodies but also of bodies pursuing delimited functions (strictly connected to the functioning of the single market). Instead, in the case of the federal union, it is necessary to go beyond the Treaty of Lisbon of 2009 and the intergovernmental treaties approved subsequently. Here, the "ever closer union" must be organized according to the logic of multiple separation of powers. The vertical separation between national and supranational levels of government and the horizontal separation between the institutions participating in the governmental process at the supranational level must be constitutionalized. To design this union, it is necessary to recall Montesquieu (1689–1755), according to whom the confusion of powers inevitably produces despotism, and James Madison (1751–1836), according to whom the paradox of a sovereign union of sovereign states can be solved only through a constitutionally protected anti-centralizing, anti-hegemonic, and anti-hierarchical governance system (Fabbrini 2010: 142–152). In this system, nonetheless, citizens must have the possibility of influencing the decisions of its political authorities by taking part in the choice of its executive and in the formation of its legislature. And at the same time, citizens must participate in the democratic process for affecting national policies. Albeit much more complex than national democracies, supranational democracy must allow citizens to influence political choices and must guarantee accountability to the citizens of those making decisions at the various levels of government. The construction of a federal union within a plural Europe will require creativity and intelligence, but above all, it will require political leadership. Federal unions are decided, not inherited. The spirit of the Manifesto of Ventotene has never been more essential in order to oppose and defeat the "holy" alliance between populism and nationalism that generated sovereignism as the modern adversary of a political Europe.

Bibliography

Amadio Viceré, M.G. (2018). *The High Representative and EU Foreign Policy Integration: A Comparative Study of Kosovo and Ukraine*, London: Palgrave Macmillan.

Amato, G. and J. Ziller (2007). *The European Constitution: Cases and Materials in EU and Member States' Law*, Cheltenham: Edward Elgar.

Barbieri, P. and S. Vallée (2017). "Europe's Hamilton Moment: A New Kind of Federalism for the Continent," *ForeignAffairs.com*, July 26.

Bastasin, C. (2015). *Saving Europe: Anatomy of a Dream*, 2nd ed. Washington, DC: Brookings Institution Press.

Beard, C.A. (ed.) (1948). *The Enduring Federalist*, New York: Frederick Ungar.

Beer, S.H. (1993). *To Make a Nation: The Rediscovery of American Federalism*, Cambridge, MA: Harvard University Press.

Bickerton, C.J. (2012). *European Integration: From Nation-States to Member States*, Oxford: Oxford University Press.

Bickerton, C.J., D. Hodson and W. Puetter (eds.) (2015). *The New Intergovernmentalism: States and Supranational Actors in the Post-Maastricht Era*, Oxford: Oxford University Press.

Borzel, T.A. (2016). "From EU Governance of Crisis to Crisis of EU Governance: Regulatory Failure, Redistributive Conflict and Eurosceptic Public," *Journal of Common Market Studies*, 54: 8–31.

Bressanelli, E. and N. Chelotti (2016). "The Shadow of the European Council: Understanding Legislation on Economic Governance," *Journal of European Integration*, 38/5: 509–524.

Brinkley, A., N.W. Polsby and K.M. Sullivan (1997). *New Federalist Papers: Essays in Defense of the Constitution*, New York: Twentieth Century Fund Book.

Brunnermeier, M.K., H. James and J.-P. Landau (2016). *The Euro and the Battle of Ideas*, Princeton, NJ: Princeton University Press.

Bruszt, L. (2017). "Regional Normalization and National Deviations: EU Integration and the Backsliding of Democracy in Europe's Eastern Periphery," Global Policy Journal, forthcoming.

Buchanan, J.M. (1965). "An Economic Theory of Clubs," *Economica*, 32/1: 1–14.

Bulmer, S. (2014). "Germany and the Eurozone Crisis: Between Hegemony and Domestic Politics," *West European Politics*, 37/6: 1244–1263.

Bulmer, S. and W.E. Paterson (2013). "Germany as the EU's Reluctant Hegemon? Of Economic Strength and Political Constraints," *Journal of European Public Policy*, 20/10: 1387–1405.

Bulmer, S. and W.E. Paterson (2010). "Germany and the European Union: From 'Tamed Power' to Normalized Power?," *International Affairs*, 86/5: 1051–1073.

Cain, B.A. (2015). *Democracy More or Less: America's Political Reform Quandary*, Cambridge: Cambridge University Press.

Calleo, D.P. (2001). *Rethinking Europe's Future*, Princeton, NJ: Princeton University Press.

Caporaso, J. (2018). "Europe's Triple Crisis," *Journal of Common Market Studies*, forthcoming.

Caporaso, J. and M. Rhodes (eds.) (2016). *The Political and Economic Dynamics of the Eurozone Crisis*, Oxford: Oxford University Press.

Carmassi, J., C. Di Noia and S. Micossi (2012). "Banking Union: A Federal Model for the European Union with Prompt Corrective Action," *Note e Studi*, Rome: Assonime.

Christiansen, T. (2016), "After the *Spitzenkandidaten*: Fundamental Change in the EU's Political System?," *West European Politics*, 39/5: 992–1010.

Clark, C. (2014). *The Sleepwalkers: How Europe Went to War in 1914*, New York: Harper Perennial.

Crabb, C.V. and P.M. Holt (1992). *An Invitation to Struggle: Congress, the President and Foreign Policy*, 4th ed. Washington, DC: CQ Press.

Craig, P. (2017). "Brexit, A Drama: The Interregnum," *Yearbook of European Law*, 56: 1–43.

Craig, P. (2011). *The Lisbon Treaty: Law, Politics and Treaty Reform*, Oxford: Oxford University Press.

Crouch, C. (2004). *Post-democracy*, Cambridge: Polity Press.

Dahl, R.A. (2006). *A Preface to Democratic Theory*, expanded edition. Chicago: University of Chicago Press, original edition 1956.

Dahl, R.A. (2003). *How Democratic Is the American Constitution?* New Haven, CT: Yale University Press.

Dehousse, R. (2016). "Why Has EU Macroeconomic Governance Become More Supranational?," *Journal of European Integration*, 38/5: 611–625.

Dehousse, R. (ed.) (2011). *The "Community Method": Obstinate or Obsolete?* New York: Palgrave Macmillan.

De Witte, B., A. Ott and E. Vos (eds.). (2017). *Between Flexibility and Disintegration: The Trajectory of Differentiation in EU Law*, Cheltenham: Edward Elgar.

Dinan, D. (2005). *Ever Closer Union. An Introduction to European Integration*, New York: Palgrave Macmillan.

Duchene, F. (1994). *Jean Monnet: The First Statesman of Interdependence*, New York: W.W. Norton.

Dyson, K. (2012). "Economic and Monetary Union," in E. Jones, A. Menon and S. Weatherill (eds.), *The Oxford Handbook of the European Union*, Oxford: Oxford University Press, pp. 453–468.

Dyson, K. (ed.) (2008). *The Euro at 10: Europeanization, Power, and Convergence*, Oxford: Oxford University Press.

Egan, M. (2015). *Single Markets: Economic Integration in Europe and the United States*, Oxford: Oxford University Press.

Elazar, D.J. (1994). *The American Mosaic: The Impact of Space, Time, and Culture on American Politics*, Boulder, CO: Westview Press.

Elazar, D.J. (1988). *The American Constitutional Tradition*, Lincoln: University of Nebraska Press.

Elazar, D.J. (1987). *Exploring Federalism*, Tuscaloosa: University of Alabama Press.

Ellis, J.J. (2015). *The Quartet: Orchestrating the Second American Revolution, 1783–1789*, New York: Random House.

Enderlein, H. and J. Haas (2015). "What Would a European Finance Minister Do? A Proposal," Policy Paper No. 145, Jacques Delors Institute, October.

Epstein, R. and M. Rhodes (2016). "International in Life, National in Death? Banking Nationalism on the Road to Banking Union," in J. Caporaso. and M. Rhodes (eds.), *The Political and Economic Dynamics of the Eurozone Crisis*, Oxford: Oxford University Press, pp. 200–232.

Eriksen, E.O. (2017). "A Segmented Political Order in Europe: Differentiated Integration and the Problem of Arbitrary Rule," paper delivered at the ECPR Conference, Oslo, September.

European Commission (2015). "Plan for Strengthening Europe's Economic and Monetary Union," Brussels, June 22.

European Council (2016). "Draft Decision of the Heads of State or Government, meeting within the European Council, concerning a New Settlement for the United Kingdom within the European Union (doc. EUCO 4/16)," Brussels, February 2.

Fabbrini, F. (ed.) (2017). *The Law and Politics of Brexit*, Oxford: Oxford University Press.

Fabbrini, F. (2016). *Economic Governance in Europe: Comparative Paradoxes, Constitutional Challenges*, Oxford: Oxford University Press.

Fabbrini, F. (2015). "After the OMT Case: The Supremacy of EU Law as the Guarantee of the Equality of the Member States," *German Law Journal*, 16/4: 1003–1024.

Fabbrini, S. (2017a). "Which Democracy for a Union of States? A Comparative Perspective of the European Union," *Global Policy*, 8/3: 14–22.

Fabbrini, S. (2017b). "Intergovernmentalism in the EU: A Comparative Federalism Perspective," *Journal of European Public Policy*, 24/4: 580–597.

Fabbrini, S. (2016a). "From Consensus to Domination: The Intergovernmental Union," *Journal of European Integration*, 38/5: 587–599.

Fabbrini, S. (2016b). "The Euro Crisis through Two Paradigms: Interpreting the Transformation of European Economic Governance," *European Politics and Society*, 18/3: 318–332.

Fabbrini, S. (2016c). "Representation without Taxation: Association or Union of States?," in A. De Feo and B. Laffan (eds.), *EU Own Resources: Momentum for a Reform?* e-book, Fiesole (Florence): European University Institute, Robert Schuman Centre for Advanced Studies, pp. 19–28.

Fabbrini, S. (2016d). "The Constitutional Conundrum of the European Union," *Journal of European Public Policy*, 23/1: 84–100.

Fabbrini, S. (2015a). *Which European Union? Europe After the Euro Crisis*, Cambridge: Cambridge University Press.

Fabbrini, S. (2015b). "The European Union and the Puzzle of Parliamentary Government," *Journal of European Integration*, 37/5: 571–586.

Fabbrini, S. (2014). "The European Union and the Libyan Crisis," *International Politics*, 51/2: 177–195.

Fabbrini, S. (2013). "Intergovernmentalism and Its Limits: Assessing the European Union's Answer to the Euro Crisis," *Comparative Political Studies*, 46/9: 1003–1029.

Fabbrini, S. (2010). *Compound Democracies: Why the United States and Europe Are Becoming Similar*, 2nd ed. Oxford: Oxford University Press.

Fabbrini, S. (2008). *America and Its Critics. Virtues and Vices of the Democratic Hyper-power*, Cambridge: Polity Press.

Fabbrini, S. and U. Puetter (eds.) (2016). "Integration without Supranationalisation: The Central Role of the European Council in Post-Lisbon EU Politics," special issue, *Journal of European Integration*, 38/5.

Ferrera, M. (2017). "Mission Impossible? Reconciling Economic and Social Europe after the Euro Crisis and Brexit," *European Journal of Political Research*, 56/1: 3–22.

Fisher, L. (2013). *Presidential War Power*, 3rd ed. Lawrence: University Press of Kansas.

Fossum, J.-E. (2015). "Democracy and Differentiation in Europe," *Journal of European Public Policy*, 22/6: 799–815.

Fossum, J.-E. and M. Jachtenfuchs (2017). "Federal Challenges and Challenges to Federalism. Insights from the EU and Federal States," *Journal of European Public Policy*, 24/4: 467–485.

Fossum, J.-E. and A.J. Menéndez (2011). *The Constitution's Gift: A Constitutional Theory for a Democratic European Union*, Lanham, MD: Rowman and Littlefield.

Fukuyama, F. (2018). *Identity: Contemporary Identity Politics and the Struggle for Recognition*, London: Profile Boks.

Fukuyama, F. (2014). *Political Order and Political Decay: From the Industrial Revolution to the Globalization of Democracy*, New York: Farrar, Straus and Giroux.

Genschel, P. and M. Jachtenfuchs. (2017). "From Market Integration to Core State Powers: The Eurozone Crisis, the Refugee Crisis and Integration Theory," *Journal of Common Market Studies*, 56/4: 1–19.

Genschel, P. and M. Jachtenfuchs (2016). "Conflict-Minimising Integration: How the EU Achieves Massive Integration Despite Massive Protest," in D. Chalmers, M. Jachtenfuchs and C. Joerges (eds.), *The End of the Eurocrats' Dream: Adjusting to European Diversity*, Cambridge: Cambridge University Press, pp. 166–189.

Genschel, P. and M. Jachtenfuchs (eds.). (2014). *Beyond the Regulatory Polity? The European Integration of Core State Powers*, Oxford: Oxford University Press.

Greenfeld, L. (2012). *Nationalism. Five Roads to Modernity*, Cambridge, MA: Harvard University Press.

Grimm, D. (2015). *Sovereignty: The Origin and Future of a Political and Legal Concept*, New York: Columbia University Press.

Habermas, J. (2012). *The Crisis of the European Union: A Response*, Oxford: Polity Press.

Hacker, B. and C.M. Koch (2017). *The Divided Eurozone: Mapping Conflicting Interests on the Reform of the Monetary Union*, Berlin: Friedrich Ebert Stiftung.

Heipertz, M. and A. Verdun (2010). *Ruling Europe: The Politics of the Stability and Growth Pact*, Cambridge: Cambridge University Press.

Hendricks, G. and A. Morgan (2001). *The Franco-German Axis in European Integration*, Cheltenham: Edward Elgar.

Hendrickson, D.C. (2009). *Union, Nation, or Empire: The American Debate Over International Relations, 1789–1941*, Lawrence: University Press of Kansas.

Hendrickson, D.C. (2003). *Peace Pact: The Lost World of the American Founding*, Lawrence: University Press of Kansas.

Henning, C.R. (2017). *Tangled Governance: International Regime Complexity, the Troika, and the Euro Crisis*, Oxford: Oxford University Press.

Henning, C.R. (2016). "The ECB as a Strategic Actor: Central Banking in a Politically Fragmented Monetary Union," in J.A. Caporaso and M. Rhodes (eds.), *Political and Economic Dynamics of the Eurozone Crisis*, Oxford: Oxford University Press, pp. 167–199.

Heritier, A. (2007). *Explaining Institutional Change in Europe*, Oxford: Oxford University Press.

Heritier, A. and M. Rhodes (eds.). (2010). *New Modes of Governance in Europe*, New York: Palgrave Macmillan.

Hix, S. (2008). "Why the EU Needs (Left-Right) Politics: Policy Reform and Accountability Are Impossible without It," Notre Europe Policy Paper No. 19, Paris, http://www.notre-europe.eu/uploads/txpublica tion/Policypaper19-en.pdf.

Hix S. and B. Hoyland. (2011). *The Political System of the European Union*, New York: Palgrave Macmillan.

Hoffman, L., C. Parsons and B. Springer (2017). "Hayek, Polany, and Single Markets (Or How Europe's Single Market Surpassed America's)," paper delivered at the Conference of the European Union Studies Association, Miami, Florida, May 4–7.

Hooghe, L. and G. Marks (2009). "A Postfunctionalist Theory of European Integration: From Permissive Consensus to Constraining Dissensus," *British Journal of Political Science*, 39/1: 1–23.

Huntington, S.P. (2004). *Who Are We? The Challenges to America's National Identity*, New York: Simon & Schuster.

Ikenberry, J.G. (2000). *After Victory: Institutions, Strategic Restraint and the Rebuilding of the Order after Major Wars*, Princeton, NJ: Princeton University Press.

Issing, O. (2008). *The Birth of the Euro*, Cambridge: Cambridge University Press.

Jachtenfuchs, M. (1995). "Theoretical Perspectives on European Governance," *European Law Journal*, 1/2: 115–133.

Jackson, J. (2003). *France: The Dark Years, 1940–1944*, Oxford: Oxford University Press.

Jacobs, L. and D. King (eds.) (2009). *The Unsustainable American State*, Oxford: Oxford University Press.

Jacoby, W. (2017). "Surplus Germany," Transatlantic Academy Paper Series, No. 8.

James, H. (2012). *Making the European Monetary Union*, Cambridge, MA: The Belknap Press of Harvard University Press.

Jarausch, K.H. (1994). *The Rush to German Unity*, Oxford: Oxford University Press.

Joerges, C. (2016). "Integration through Law and the Crisis of Law in Europe's Emergency," in D. Chalmers, M. Jachtenfuchs and C. Joerges (eds.), *The End of the Eurocrats' Dream: Adjusting to European Diversity*, Cambridge: Cambridge University Press, pp. 299–338.

Jones, E. (2015). "The Forgotten Financial Union: How You Can Have a Euro Crisis without a Euro," in M. Matthijs and M. Blyth (eds.), *The Future of the Euro*, Oxford: Oxford University Press, pp. 44–69.

Jones, E., R.D. Kelemen and S. Meunier (2016). "Failing Forward? The Euro Crisis and the Incomplete Nature of European Integration," *Comparative Political Studies*, 49/7: 1010–1034.

Judis, J.B. (2016). *The Populist Explosion: How the Great Recession Transformed American and European Politics*, New York: Columbia Global Reports.

Judt, T. (2005). *Postwar. A History of Europe Since 1945*, London: Penguin Books.

Juncker, J.-C. et al. (2015). "Completing Europe's Economic and Monetary Union," report prepared by the President of the Commission, in collaboration with the President of the Council of Europe, the President of the Eurogroup, the President of the European Central Bank and the President of the European Parliament, June.

Katznelson, I. and M. Shefter (eds.) (2002). *Shaped by War and Trade: International Influences on American Political Development*, Princeton, NJ: Princeton University Press.

Kelemen, R.D. (2019). "Is Differentiation Possible in Rule of Law?" *Comparative European Politics*, forthcoming.

Kelemen, R.D. (2015). "Europe's Hungary Problems: Viktor Orban Flouts the Union," Foreign Affairs, March–April.

Kelemen, R.D. (2014). "Building the New European State? Federalism, Core State Powers, and European Integration," in P. Genschel and M. Jachtenfuchs (eds.), *Beyond the Regulatory Polity? The European Integration of Core State Powers*: Oxford: Oxford University Press, pp. 211–229.

Kelemen, R.D. (2011). *Eurolegalism: The Transformation of Law and Regulation in the European Union*, Cambridge, MA: Harvard University Press.

Kelemen, R.D. and K. Nicolaidis (2007). "Bringing Federalism Back In," in K.E. Jorgensen, M. Pollack and B. Rosamond (eds.), *Handbook of European Union Politics*, London: Sage, pp. 301–316.

Kissinger, H.A. (1956). "The Congress of Vienna: A Reappraisal," *World Politics*, 8/2: 264–280.

Klarman, M.J. (2016). *The Framers' Coup: The Making of the United States Constitution*, Oxford: Oxford University Press.

Krastev, I. (2017). *After Europe*, Philadelphia: University of Pennsylvania Press.

Kreppel, A. and B. Oztas. (2016). "Leading the Band or Just Playing the Tune? Reassessing the Agenda-Setting Power of the European Commission," *Comparative Political Studies*, 50/8: 1118–1150.

Kupchan, C.A. (ed.) (1995). *Nationalism and Nationalities in the New Europe*, Ithaca, NY: Cornell University Press.

Lacroix, J. (2010). "Borderline Europe: French Visions of the European Union," in J. Lacroix and K. Nicolaidis (eds.), *European Stories: Intellectual Debates on Europe in National Context*, Oxford: Oxford University Press, pp. 105–121.

Lacroix, J. and K. Nicolaidis (eds.). (2010). *European Stories: Intellectual Debates on Europe in National Context*, Oxford: Oxford University Press.

Laffan, B. (2014). "Testing Times: The Growing Primacy of Responsibility in the Euro Area," *West European Politics* 37/2: 270–287.

Leuffen, D., B. Rittberger and F. Schimmelfennig (2013). *Differentiated Integration: Explaining Variation in the European Union*, New York: Palgrave Macmillan.

Lijphart, A. (1999). *Patterns of Democracy*, New Haven, CT: Yale University Press.

Lindberg, L.N. (1963). *The Political Dynamics of European Economic Integration*, Stanford, CA: Stanford University Press.

Mair, P. (2013). *Ruling the Void: The Hollowing of Western Democracy*, London: Verso.

Majone, G. (2014). *Rethinking the Union of Europe Post-Crisis: Has Integration Gone Too Far?* Cambridge: Cambridge University Press.

Matthijs, M. (2017). "Europe after Brexit: A Less Perfect Union," *Foreign Affairs*, January–February, 85–95.

Matthijs, M. (2016). "Powerful Rules Governing the Euro: The Perverse Power and Logic of German Ideas," *Journal of European Public Policy*, 23/3: 375–391.

Matthijs, M. and M. Blyth (eds.) (2015). *The Future of the Euro*, Oxford: Oxford University Press.

McNamara, K.R. (2017). *The Politics of Everyday Europe: Constructing Authority in the European Union*, Oxford: Oxford University Press.

Megan, G. and R.D. Kelemen (2016). "Europe's Lousy Deal with Turkey: Why the Refugee Arrangement Won't Work," *ForeignAffairs.com*, March 29.

Mény, Y. (2014). "Managing the EU Crises: Another Way of Integration by Stealth?," *West European Politics*, 37/6: 1336–1353.

Mény, Y. and Y. Surel (2000). *Par le peuple, pour le peuple. Le populisme et les démocraties*, Paris: Fayard.

Merritt, G. (2016). *Slippery Slope: Europe's Troubled Future*, Oxford: Oxford University Press.

Moury, C. (2007). "Explaining the European Parliament's Right to Appoint and Invest the Commission," *West European Politics*, 30/2: 367–391.

Mudde, C. (2016). "Europe's Populist Surge," *Foreign Affairs*, November–December, 25–30.

Mueller, J.-W. (2016). *What Is Populism?* Philadelphia: University of Pennsylvania Press.

Mueller, J.-W. (2010). "In the Shadows of Statism: Peculiarities of the German Debates on European Integration," in J. Lacroix, and K. Nicolaidis (eds.), *European Stories: Intellectual Debates on Europe in National Context*, Oxford: Oxford University Press, pp. 87–104.

Neustadt, R.E. (1990). *Presidential Power and the Modern President: The Politics of Leadership from Roosevelt to Reagan*, 3rd ed. New York: The Free Press.

Neyer, J. (2015). "Empowering the Sovereign: National Parliaments in European Union Monetary and Financial Policy," in S. Piattoni (ed.), *The European Union: Democratic Principles and Institutional Architectures in Times of Crisis*, Oxford: Oxford University Press, pp. 219–235.

Nicolaidis, K. (2013). "European Democracy and Its Crises," *Journal of Common Market Studies*, 51/2: 351–369.

Nicolaidis, K., B. Sèbe and G. Mass (eds.) (2015). *Echoes of Empire: Memory, Identity and Colonial Legacies*, London: I.B. Tauris.

Norman, P. (2003). *The Accidental Constitution. The Story of the European Convention*, Brussels: Eurocomment.

Onuf, P.S. (1983). *The Origins of the Federal Republic: Jurisdictional Controversies in the United States, 1775–1787*, Philadelphia: University of Pennsylvania Press.

Orren, K. and S. Skowroneck (2017). *The Policy State: An American Predicament*, Cambridge, MA: Harvard University Press.

Ostrom, V. (1991). *The Meaning of American Federalism: Constituting a Self-Governing Society*, San Francisco: Institute of Contemporary Studies.

Ostrom, V. (1987). *The Political Theory of a Compound Republic: Designing the American Experiment*, 2nd ed. Lincoln: University of Nebraska Press.

Parsons, C. and M. Matthijs (2015). "European Integration Past, Present and Future: Moving Forward through Crisis?," in M. Matthijs and M. Blyth (eds.), *The Future of the Euro*, Oxford: Oxford University Press, pp. 210–232.

Piattoni, S. (2015). "The European Union: Legitimating Values, Democratic Principles, and Institutional Architectures," in S. Piattoni (ed.), *The European Union: Democratic Principles and Institutional*

Architectures in Times of Crisis, Oxford: Oxford University Press, pp. 3–25.

Piris, J.C. (2012). *The Future of Europe: Towards a Two-Speed EU*, Cambridge: Cambridge University Press.

Polsby, N.W. (2008). "The Political System," in P.H. Schuck and J.Q. Wilson (eds.), *Understanding America: The Anatomy of an Exceptional Nation*, New York: Public Affairs, pp. 3–26.

Puetter, U. (2014). *The European Council and the Council: New Intergovernmentalism and Institutional Change*, Oxford: Oxford University Press.

Puetter, U. (2012). "Europe's Deliberative Intergovernmentalism: The Role of the Council and European Council in EU Economic Governance," *Journal of European Public Policy*, 19/2: 161–178.

Puetter, U. (2006). *The Eurogroup: How a Secretive Circle of Finance Ministers Shape European Economic Governance*, Manchester: Manchester University Press.

Riker, W. (1975). "Federalism," in F. Greenstein and N. Polsby (eds.), *Handbook of Political Science*, Vol. 5. Reading, MA.: Addison-Wesley, pp. 93–172.

Risse, T. (2010). *A Community of Europeans? Transnational Identities and Public Spheres*, Ithaca, NY: Cornell University Press.

Rittberger, B. (2005). *Building Europe's Parliament: Democratic Representation beyond the Nation-State*, Oxford: Oxford University Press.

Rittberger, B. (2003). "The Creation and Empowerment of the European Parliament," *Journal of Common Market Studies*, 41/2: 2013–2026.

Rodrik, D. (2011). *The Globalization Paradox: Democracy and the Future of the World Economy*, New York: W.W. Norton.

Rodrik, D. (2007). *The Inescapable Trilemma of the World Economy*, Weblog, June 27.

Sbragia, A.M. (1994). "From Nation-State to Member State: The Evolution of the European Community," in P.M. Lutzeler (ed.), *Europe after Maastricht: American and European Perspectives*, Oxford: Berghahn Books, pp. 69–87.

Sbragia, A.M. (1992). "Thinking About the European Future: The Uses of Comparison," in A.M. Sbragia (ed.), *Euro-Politics: Institutions and Policy-Making in the New European Community*, Washington, DC: Brookings Institution Press, pp. 257–291.

Scharpf, F.W. (2016). "The Costs of Non-disintegration: The Case of the European Monetary Union," in D. Chalmers, M. Jachtenfuchs and C. Joerges (eds.), *The End of the Eurocrats' Dream: Adjusting to European Diversity*, Cambridge: Cambridge University Press, pp. 29–49.

Scharpf, F.W. (2009). "Legitimacy in the Multilevel European Polity," *European Political Science Review*, 1/2: 173–204.

Scharpf, F.W. (2008). "Community, Diversity and Autonomy: The Challenges of Reforming German Federalism," *German Politics*, 17/4: 509–521.

Schauble, W. (2012). "Perfekte Losungen brauchen lange," interview with W. Schauble by B. Sven and G. Thesing, *Der* Spiegel, June 25.

Schelkle, W. (2017). *The Political Economy of Monetary Solidarity: Understanding the Euro Experiment*, Oxford: Oxford University Press.

Schimmelfennig, F. (2018). "European Integration (Theory) in Times of Crisis. A Comparison of the Euro and Schengen Crises," *Journal of European Public Policy*, 25/7: 969–989.

Schmidt, V. (2016). "Reinterpreting the Rules 'by Stealth' in Times of Crisis: The European Central Bank and the European Commission," *West European Politics*, 39/5: 1032–1052.

Schmidt, V. (2015). "The Forgotten Problem of Legitimacy: 'Governing by the Rules' and 'Ruling by the Numbers,'" in M. Matthijs and M. Blyth (eds.), *The Future of the Euro*, Oxford: Oxford University Press, pp. 90–114.

Schutze, R. (2010). *From Dual to Cooperative Federalism*, Oxford: Oxford University Press.

Skowroneck, S. (1982). *Building a New American State: The Expansion of National Administration Capacities, 1877–1920*, Cambridge: Cambridge University Press.

Spruyt, H. (1994). *The Sovereign State and Its Competitors*, Princeton, NJ: Princeton University Press.

Stepan, A.C. (1999). "Federalism and Democracy: Beyond the US Model," *Journal of Democracy*, 10/4: 19–34.

Stone Sweet, A. (2000). *Governing with Judges: Constitutional Politics in Europe*, Oxford: Oxford University Press.

Stone Sweet, A., Sandholtz, W. and Fligstein, N. (eds.) (2001). *The Institutionalization of Europe*, Oxford: Oxford University Press.

Sugar, P.F. (1994). *Eastern European Nationalism in the Twentieth Century*, Lanham, MD: University Press of America.

Tsoukalis, L. (2016). *In Defence of Europe: Can the European Project Be Saved?* Oxford: Oxford University Press.

Tuori, K. and K. Tuori (2014). *The Eurozone Crisis: A Constitutional Analysis*, Cambridge: Cambridge University Press.

Van Rompuy, H. (2012). "Towards a Genuine Economic and Monetary Union," report prepared by the President of the Council of Europe, in collaboration with the President of the Commission, the President of the Eurogroup and the President of the European Central Bank, December.

Veron, N. (2015). *Europe's Radical Banking Union,* Bruegel Essay and Lecture Series, Brussels.

Walker, N. (2004). "The EU as a Constitutional Project," *The Federal Trust,* 19, http://www.fedetrust.co.uk/uploads/constitution/19_04.pdf.

Wallace, P. (2016). *The Euro Experiment,* Cambridge: Cambridge University Press.

Walzer, M. (1996). *What It Means to Be an American: Essays on the American Experience,* New York: Marsilio.

Weiler, J.H.H. (2000). "Federalism and Constitutionalism: Europe's Sonderweg," Harvard Law School, Jean Monnet Chair Working Papers, http://ftp.infoeuropa.eurocid.pt/fi les/database/ 000036001–000037000/000036583.pdf.

Weiler, J.H.H. (1999). *The Constitution of Europe,* Cambridge: Cambridge University Press.

Wessels, W. (2015). *The European Council,* New York: Palgrave Macmillan.

Wessels, W. (1997). "An Ever Closer Fusion? A Dynamic Macropolitical View on Integration Processes," *Journal of Common Market Studies,* 35/2: 267–299.

Woodard, C. (2012). *American Nations: A History of the Eleven Rival Regional Cultures of North America,* New York: Penguin Books.

Wozniakowski, T.P. (2017). "Why the Sovereign Debt Crisis Could Lead to a Federal Fiscal Union: The Paradoxical Origins of Fiscalization in the United States and Insights for the European Union," Journal of European Public Policy, http://dx.doi.org/10.1080/13501763.2017.1285340.

Zielonka, J. (2014). *Is the EU Doomed?* Cambridge: Polity Press.

Index